A HARD CELL

BOB BATES

A HARD CELL

MY INCARCERATION AND THE PRISON CONDITIONS THAT ALMOST ENDED MY LIFE

Copyright © 2020 by Bob Bates.

All rights reserved. No part of this book may be used or reproduced in any manner whatsoever without prior written consent of the author, except as provided by the United States of America copyright law.

Printed in the United States of America.

10 9 8 7 6 5 4 3 2 1

ISBN: 978-1-94963-985-8
LCCN: 2020900669

Cover design by Jamie Wise.
Layout design by Wesley Strickland.

This publication is designed to provide accurate and authoritative information in regard to the subject matter covered. It is sold with the understanding that the publisher is not engaged in rendering legal, accounting, or other professional services. If legal advice or other expert assistance is required, the services of a competent professional person should be sought.

First, I would like to thank my wife, Charlotte, for always being in my corner during the most difficult times in my life. I am so grateful to my daughters, Leslie McCrary and Kathy Walter, and their families for their tremendous support through our ordeal. I would not have made it through without the continuous visits from my amazing family! Thank you for everything! I love you!

CONTENTS

ACKNOWLEDGMENTS
FROM CHARLOTTE ix

CHAPTER

1 1

CHAPTER

2 13

CHAPTER

3 25

CHAPTER

4 33

CHAPTER

5 43

CHAPTER

6 59

CHAPTER

7 87

CHAPTER
8
103

CHAPTER
9
125

CHAPTER
10
141

CHAPTER
11
151

CHAPTER
12
165

CHAPTER
13
181

CHAPTER
14
197

CHAPTER
15
207

ACKNOWLEDGMENTS FROM CHARLOTTE

FIRST AND FOREMOST, we owe our hearts and thanks to our Lord and Savior Jesus Christ. Without His protection and love, we would have never made it through this horrible ordeal!

To our girls, Leslie and Kathy, who were such a force of strength, love, and compassion. Through endless hours of what we thought would never end, the thousands of miles driven, the tears, fights, laughter, fear, and our love and support for your dad! I am so thankful for you precious ladies. I am proud to call you my daughters. I thank you from the bottom and top of my heart! We love you both so much!

To my sister, Terrie Atchison, who was with us from day one. Through the trial, the sentencing, and prison, my best friend was there for us. During my darkest hours, you were my strength! I could not have made it through this nightmare without you. I love you today, tomorrow, and forever!

Thank you, Jerry Atchison, for listening to me cry every single night and feeding me! I love you!

To my other sister and best friend, Sheila Landry. I truly do not know what I would have done without you. Endless phone calls from me in the middle of the night, crying and needing a friend to listen. Sheila, you were always there for me! I love you forever!

To my longest best friend of forty-five years, Tamra Sheehan. We have been through so much together! You were always there for me with words of encouragement, support, and love. Truly a godsend! Thank you so much for believing the truth and letting others know. I love you always!

To my dear friend Connie B. Taverner for keeping us in her prayers and heart. Connie, you helped me stay in communication with people when I wanted to crawl into a hole and stay there! Thank you so very much! I love you, girl!

To our wonderful friends Debbie and David Morris. We cannot begin to thank you enough for all of your support, love, and friendship for so many years. You are truly wonderful people who have always been there for Bob and me. There are not enough words to express our gratitude! We love and cherish our friendship more than you know.

To Julie Bates, Bob's precious sister. Thank you for fighting day in and day out, seeking justice for your brother and for writing letters to him that helped heal the loneliness. You are an amazing woman and sister. We love you so very much, and we thank you from our hearts.

To all our family: Jim McCrary, Bobby McCrary, Sam McCrary, Julianne McCrary, Jim Walter, Reece Walter, Paul Walter, Jack Walter, Tyler Pack, Rick and Nancy Richards, Travis and Lydia Richards, Sean Fidler, Treavor and Loretta Richards, Ferrial Richards, Little Travis Richards, and my precious mother and dad.

To my neighbors John and Sandy Stava for always thinking of me on holidays, bringing me food, flowers, and prayers for Bob and me.

I am so blessed to know you.

ACKNOWLEDGMENTS FROM CHARLOTTE

Thank you to all of our neighbors who stood with us through this nightmare. Thank you to our dear friends Beverly and Scott Good. Your undying friendship through the darkest hours was such a blessing. We love you!

To the ladies at Bob's office for their ceaseless loyalty and support.

To Brian Connally, for making me laugh during some really dark days. Thank you for helping me keep everything together.

To Bill and Ann Page, Bob's wonderful friends since junior high. Thank you for calling and helping me through some really rough times.

To the juror who knew right from wrong and wrote the judge to tell him there had been a terrible mistake in Bob's verdict. For standing up for truth and justice.

To all of the good people and friends who wrote letters to the judge asking for grace and no jail time for Bob.

To Mr. Kinnison, thank you for your kindness.

To the prisoners, thank you!

To our lawyers, Clark and Corbin Brewster, and the whole team that fought THE PERFECT STORM no human could have won! Thank you for believing in Bob and working so hard for his freedom.

Thank you to Steve for spending hours with Bob and me talking about this horrible ordeal and for helping us put our story and feelings into this book.

It is hard for me to put into words the heartfelt admiration and respect we have for a very special doctor. Dr. Fred McNeer fought from the very beginning of Bob's incarceration for the humane treatment of prisoners. He was appalled and shocked at the inexcusable and inhumane treatment of Bob at David Moss Correctional Center. Dr. McNeer fought hard to help Bob get what was denied him as a prisoner in that jail: basic needs and medications. We are forever grateful to this truly amazing man.

A very important thank you to Pastor Chris Thompson. I truly don't know what we would have done without you! From the beginning of this nightmare, you were right by our side. Bringing Bob his Bible and the much-needed visits in jail and prison were so appreciated.

You truly are a man of God.

And finally, thank you to my husband, Bob, for giving up his freedom for the principles he strongly believes in, for fighting the war on drugs, and for helping to make our community safe.

Thank you for showing me the true strength of the human mind and spirit.

And, most of all, thank you for coming home to me and our dogs … alive.

1

THE FOLLOWING STORY was published in the April 28, 2016, edition of the *Tulsa World*:

Robert Bates Convicted of Manslaughter in Shooting of Eric Harris

By Arianna Pickard & Corey Jones, World Staff Writers

A jury spent less than three hours deliberating Wednesday to decide that Robert Bates was criminally negligent and deserves criminal punishment for shooting and killing an unarmed suspect while on duty as a Tulsa County Sheriff's Office reserve deputy last year.

Jurors recommended the maximum sentence of four years in prison after finding Bates guilty of second-degree manslaughter for mistaking his revolver for his Taser and shooting Eric Harris.

Bates, 74, didn't show much emotion but stroked his chin after he heard the verdict and waited to be taken from the courtroom.

The room was filled beyond capacity with spectators and 12 deputies, and District Judge William Musseman said he would hold in contempt anyone who reacted audibly to the verdict.

Bates softly told family members he loved them as a deputy escorted him, handcuffed, from the courtroom to be taken to the Tulsa Jail, where he will be held without bail until he is formally sentenced on May 31. Bates had been out of custody on bond as his case progressed through the courts.

Local and national media merely caught a glimpse of him as deputies led him out a side door.

Tulsa County Sheriff's Office spokeswoman Casey Roebuck told reporters security officers wanted to lessen Bates' exposure for his safety.

"We wanted to make sure he wasn't getting special treatment, but we also wanted to make sure that his life wasn't in danger," Roebuck said.

In the courtroom after Musseman read the verdict, Harris' sister-in-law visibly wept and was held by her husband, Andre Harris.

"I love (my brother) with all my heart, and now (Aidan Fraley) doesn't have a dad," Andre Harris told reporters afterward. "But we put the criminal behind bars."

The defense had called an out-of-state psychiatrist to testify that Bates mistakenly shooting Harris was reasonable given the stress of the situation, and before closing arguments jurors were instructed on the statutory requirements for "excusable homicide."

But after hearing from 21 witnesses in the 1 1/2 week-long trial, jurors apparently agreed with prosecutors who asserted that Bates' failure to exercise reasonable caution when he shot Harris constitutes criminal negligence.

CHAPTER 1

Within seconds of selling a gun to an undercover deputy on April 2, 2015, Harris was on the ground being restrained by multiple deputies when he was shot by Bates, witnesses testified.

"He shouldn't have even been there," Assistant District Attorney John David Luton told jurors in his closing argument.

Deputies testified that the next morning, while awaiting the signal that deputies were ready to arrest the felon they'd been warned was dangerous and likely armed, they saw Bates nodding off in his personal vehicle.

As multiple deputies struggled to restrain Harris on the ground after a short pursuit, Bates approached holding a nonlethal weapon in one hand and a lethal one in the other, Luton reminded jurors.

Seeing a small area of Harris' body where he wasn't covered by deputies, Bates announced that he was going to use his Taser and shot a bullet that struck Harris inches from another deputy's head, witnesses testified.

And despite hours of technical medical testimony from the defense, the jury agreed that the bullet killed Harris.

Luton said after the trial that despite the abundance of expert testimony, he thought "common sense" was probably what "carried the day."

Bates was convicted by a jury with no African American members. During the final stage of jury selection last week, the last two African American potential jurors were eliminated from the pool after the judge agreed that the defense had given "race-neutral" reasons for their excusal.

When asked whether he was satisfied with the jury's sentence recommendation, Andre Harris said four years in prison would "teach him (Bates) a lesson."

"That place ain't that nice," Andre Harris told reporters.

He said he hopes Bates learns that all lives matter, and he said Bates should not have been on a drug task force chasing supposedly deadly criminals.

"Not at 73," Andre Harris emphasized. "Not at 73."

He cited the 2009 Sheriff's Office internal investigation involving Bates, which contained allegations of falsified training records, intimidation of subordinates, and special treatment that benefited the insurance executive.

Looking back at the county's changes prompted by exposure to the inner workings of the Sheriff's Office, Andre Harris told reporters that his brother "accomplished a lot in his death. I think maybe even more than he accomplished in his life."

Harris' death snowballed into a wide-reaching scandal that largely emptied the top shelf of the Stanley Glanz administration at the Sheriff's Office. Glanz himself resigned from his longtime position as sheriff following a grand jury's scathing accusation for his ouster and two indictments on misdemeanor crimes.

"He's going to be remembered as a guy who helped change the city for the better," Andre Harris said. "He'll be a guy who helped change the sheriff's department and helped to better the city in general, basically."

CHAPTER 1

Assistant District Attorney Kevin Gray clarified to reporters afterward that prosecutors sought "justice" rather than "victory" because this was a case with "no winners."

"Mr. Bates had a long career and was a successful businessman, and now he will be a convicted felon who's going to the penitentiary," Gray said. "For the Harris family, they lost somebody they loved."

Bates' attorney Clark Brewster told the Tulsa World by telephone that the "massive amount" of negative media reports his client attracted in the past year generated an "uphill battle" and "created a climate in which it was virtually impossible to defend (Bates)."

Brewster said he disagrees with the jury's decision and will evaluate appeal options.

"We certainly are obviously fresh from the verdict, so we need to understand more about our options going forward," he said.

* * *

"Please rise and face the jury."

How many times had I heard those words at the movies or on TV? Probably hundreds, even thousands, of times.

But I never imagined that a judge would say them to me.

"We find the defendant guilty."

I never imagined I'd hear those words either.

But I did.

My name is Robert Bates. I shot Eric Harris, and he died.

There's a videotape of the shooting—it's easy to find on YouTube—where you can hear me say, "Oh, I shot him. I'm sorry." And I am. I was sorry then, and I'm sorry now—because I never intended to shoot Eric Harris.

And yet, I shot him. I was a volunteer reserve deputy with the Tulsa Sheriff's Department, stationed in my car as part of a drug and gun sting operation. Eric Harris ran directly toward me, trying to escape. The deputies caught him, but he was resisting arrest.

I got out of my car and reached for my Taser. But I grabbed the wrong weapon. I pulled out my gun.

> **I am a white man. Eric Harris was a black man. My timing couldn't have been worse.**

It was a mistake, but I shot him. And he died.

I shot him on April 2, 2016—just eight months after a white police officer shot an unarmed black man in Ferguson, Missouri, a shooting that sparked days of unrest in the St. Louis suburb and launched the Black Lives Matter movement across the country.

I am a white man. Eric Harris was a black man. My timing couldn't have been worse.

Police tactics when approaching or pursuing black suspects had become a major topic of discussion throughout the country, and my case quickly became national news. Matt Lauer interviewed me on *The Today Show*. Whoopi Goldberg discussed my case on *The View*. The Rev. Al Sharpton came to Tulsa to participate in protests outside the courthouse. Every major American newspaper, every broadcast network, CNN, MSNBC, Fox News … everybody wanted a piece of Bob Bates.

I was a most unlikely killer: a white-haired, seventy-four-year-old insurance executive who came out of college hoping to join the FBI. A man who spent most of his adult life working hand in hand with law enforcement. A man who donated countless thousands of dollars' worth of cars and equipment to his hometown sheriff's department.

CHAPTER 1

All of a sudden, I'd unintentionally become a very unwilling celebrity.

* * *

And that's why I found myself standing in a courtroom with jelly legs on April 28, 2016, listening to the verdict that would send me to prison.

How did that feel? I hardly remember. I can't tell you, because my mind shut down. Maybe that's something that happens at times like that. Maybe that's how we cope. But my wife, Charlotte, remembers the day in vivid detail. I'll let her describe it:

> *The morning that we knew the verdict was going to come in, we were standing in our bathroom in our home in Tulsa. Bob looked at me, and he said, "Do you think they're going to find me guilty?"*
>
> *"Absolutely not," I said. "You made a mistake, but you're not going to prison."*
>
> *He held on to me and told me, "I love you." He said, "If this thing goes wrong, I should be out in twenty-four hours, because they'll let me out on bond."*

* * *

Charlotte, her sister Terrie, and I drove to the Tulsa courthouse. I knew the place well, because I'd helped arrest dozens of suspects over the years. We went to a judge's private chambers, and we waited with our daughters and my lawyers for the jury to reach its verdict. I wanted it to come fast. The case had been dogging me for a year, and I wanted more than anything to get it behind me and move on. I was innocent. I was sure of that, and I expected the jury to agree.

While we waited, one of my lawyers, Corbin Brewster, came over and told me to go to the bathroom and clean out my pockets. He wanted me to give everything to Charlotte, just in case.

That's when it struck me for the first time: I might be found guilty.

* * *

CHARLOTTE: *Bob was very … it was like he was not in belief that anything was going to happen. Our lawyers had assured us, over and over and over again, that he would not go to prison, that there was no way possible.*

He was in total, total shock. Before he went in for the verdict, I said, "Are you OK?" He said, "Yes. I just want this over with. I wish they'd just hurry up and come back."

Then Corbin Brewster came in and called him over to the side and made Bob take all the stuff out of his pockets. I could tell by the look on Corbin's face that something was wrong, and Bob could too. He said to me, "I don't think this thing's going to go well."

I said, "Why are you saying that? Did Corbin say something?"

"No," Bob said. "I just have a bad feeling."

I said, "It's going to be OK." I was trying to comfort him. He was so stressed out.

* * *

The jury deliberated for three hours. When we were told they'd reached a verdict, we headed to the courtroom.

The place was mobbed, and they made us go through a metal detector. I'd never seen that before. I'm pretty sure it was a first in Tulsa. In fact, it may have been a first for the entire state of Oklahoma.

What did it mean? It meant they were afraid someone might try to kill me.

But I still thought I'd go free. My car was parked across the street, and I expected to walk out of the courtroom after the verdict, get into the driver's seat and leave this nightmare behind in my rearview mirror.

And now I was seated with my lawyers in front of a judge.

"Please rise and face the jury."

I did as I was told.

"We find the defendant guilty."

* * *

I was still standing in my business suit when three or four deputies—guys I knew, guys I'd helped fight crime—came up and put me in handcuffs. They put leg irons on me. They put a chain around my waist that had a black box on it so they could chain my hands down.

I had a deputy on my left and one on my right. They grabbed my arms and escorted me out of the courtroom.

* * *

CHARLOTTE: *I remember when they had him stand up. The judge told us, "If any of you make any remarks or say anything when this verdict is read, you will be in contempt of court, and we will put you in jail."*

They read the verdict, and Bob just stood there. I mean, he stood there in total shock.

Bob took it like a man when they put chains on him. They just hauled him out of there in front of us. We couldn't speak to him at all.

He just looked at me and said, "I love you."

* * *

They whisked me out of the courtroom, took me down an elevator that I'd been on many times, and then down the stairs and into a car that took me to the Tulsa County Jail, another place I knew all too well because I'd booked a lot of people into it.

They took me inside, fingerprinted me, took my mugshot, searched me. I was in shock. I didn't know what to think. I'd spent decades working with law enforcement officers in Tulsa, and now I was going to prison.

And I also wouldn't be going home on bond in twenty-four hours.

* * *

CHARLOTTE: *We didn't know until that moment that there's no bond when a gun is used. They will not bond anybody out. You can kill somebody with an ax, and you get out on bond. But if you use a gun, there's no bond.*

All I could do was tell Bob, "It's going to be OK."

Bob would get up in the wee hours of the morning to go break down meth labs. He would come home, and his skin would be crawling because meth got all over him. He helped the little children that were in these meth labs. He just did so many wonderful things ... and then, all of a sudden, he's going to prison.

* * *

I was convicted of manslaughter and sentenced to four years in prison. Because I was a first-time offender, I was released after serving eighteen months.

But I came out a changed man.

I've been called trigger happy. I've been called a racist, a vigilante, a wealthy old guy playing cop. I can't stop people from calling me whatever they choose, but I know who I am. I'm a man who made a mistake and went to prison for it. And I've had a front-row seat to witness so many things that are wrong with our criminal justice system.

I've seen how the press can prejudice a trial, how a man can be convicted by the public before a jury is so much as seated to hear his

CHAPTER 1

case. I've seen how facts can be distorted. I've seen how evidence can "disappear." Most important, I've seen how prisons are designed to dehumanize human beings.

And that's why I'm writing this book. It's not to retry myself. It's not to be found not guilty in retrospect. What happened, happened. What's done is done. I served my time, and I can't get it back.

But I never got to speak at my trial. Yes, I had the opportunity, and I declined it. But no lawyer worth his salt allows his client to take the stand in a murder trial.

* * *

I want to tell the story of my life, what brought me to the scene of the shooting, and the events of my trial. But what I want most is to tell what I experienced in court and in prison, and how and why Charlotte and I are dedicating ourselves to improving the judicial and correctional systems that fail everyone who gets caught up in them.

I want to help set a better course for others who have been abused and mishandled by the media, the court system, and the prison system—but who don't have the resources to speak out and do something about it. Yes, many of them have committed horrible crimes. But most of them will get out of jail someday, and we seem to be doing everything we can to guarantee that they'll fail on the outside and end up going back.

Criminals need to spend some time in prison, but they need to be treated humanely while they're there. They need health care; they need education; they need a chance to learn and grow. It is in our best interest to make sure that when they get out, they are not filled with bitterness and hate.

* * *

Think about this for a minute:

Eric Harris, the man I shot, was a lifelong criminal. He was forty-four years old, and he'd spent his whole life in and out of prison. If there had been programs in place to wean him off drugs, to educate him, to prepare him to survive once he was released, Eric Harris might not have been on a track to return to prison.

> In my eighteen months behind bars, I saw things I never could have imagined.

And I would not have been there to accidentally shoot him.

None of it had to happen.

This old white man, convicted of killing a black man, made some lifelong friends in prison. Some were white, some were black, some were Latino, but we all faced the same filthy conditions, unhealthy food, horrible medical care, and a denial of decency that no human being should experience, no matter what crime he has committed.

In my eighteen months behind bars, I saw things I never could have imagined.

You don't know what it's like until you've been there, and I'm living proof that you *could* be there.

Things happen in life. You can be driving your car and accidentally hit someone—maybe a kid—riding a bicycle. You might know you're innocent, but a jury might disagree.

I never had so much as a traffic ticket in my whole life. My record was spotless. I tried to help my community, and I ended up in prison.

It could happen to anyone. But what happens once you're in there should happen to no one.

2

MY NAME WASN'T ALWAYS Robert Charles Bates, and I am not a native Oklahoman.

But those are just technicalities.

I was given the name Andrew Anderson when I was born, in Kansas City, Missouri, in 1941.

But I don't remember anyone ever calling me Andy.

My parents, Leslie and Mary Bates, adopted me soon after my birth. They gave me the only name I've ever known, and they brought me to their home in Tulsa, the city I would grow up in and call my hometown.

My dad, an electrical engineer, worked for the local electric utility. My mother, a registered nurse and a social worker, became a stay-at-home mom for me and my sister, Julie, whom they adopted a few years later. It wasn't until I was twelve or thirteen that my mom went back to work for the county health department, providing care for alcoholics and drug addicts.

Our parents raised us well.

Julie grew up to become a social worker and therapist, helping transplant patients cope with their health issues at the Mayo Clinic in Scottsdale, Arizona.

I worked briefly after college as a law enforcement officer, I attended law school for a while, then I went into the insurance business. I started my own company in 1977.

* * *

We lived in the Brookside area of Tulsa, near Peoria Street, which locals called—and still call—the Restless Ribbon. If you've ever seen the movie *American Graffiti*, then you've been there. Tulsa's Restless Ribbon was just like that. And just like in the movie, there was a policeman who cruised the neighborhood, trying to keep us kids on the straight and narrow—a job too big for any cop, except Bill Willbanks wasn't just any cop.

Bill was an exceptional police officer, the only detective Tulsa had at night. And if not for him, I might never have considered a career in law enforcement.

I got to know Bill while I was a student at Thomas Edison High School. He was only about ten years older than I was—he started with the police department when he was eighteen.

I stayed in touch with him after I graduated in 1959 and headed off to Northeastern Oklahoma State University, in Tahlequah. It was only an eighty-minute drive from Tulsa, and I went home a lot on weekends. There were two reasons for that: one was Francey, my girlfriend, who was still in high school. The other was Bill Willbanks, who was becoming a good friend of mine.

Whenever I was home, Bill would let me ride with him on patrol. I was thinking about going into the police department after college, and he was becoming my mentor. We patrolled the area in a plain car, and some of our rides were unforgettable.

I remember one night a car drove past us with its interior lights on, and Bill said, "There goes a car we're gonna stop." He could just tell that something was wrong.

There were two guys in the car. We pulled it over, and the back was loaded with car parts. I handcuffed the pair and put them in our car, and we sent some patrol officers down the street to look around. It turned out that they had just broken into a mechanic's facility and taken everything they could. And if not for Bill's intuition, they might have gotten away with it.

Bill was a great role model. Back then, if somebody died outside the care of a doctor, the police department had to dispatch someone to examine the body. It wasn't the most pleasant assignment, but Bill was a professional. He was extremely thorough, opening mouths, looking for every possible clue.

He ended up running the department's training facility before he retired. I found out later that his IQ was over 160. He was definitely not your average cop.

He was a lawyer too. He went to law school at the same time I did—but he finished. He never practiced law, however, except for friends.

* * *

With Bill as my mentor, I became an auxiliary policeman, riding many nights with him and some other patrol officers.

I'd stay out very late on runs, and then I'd go home and sleep for an hour or two, because I had to get up and work at a gas station for $1.10 an hour.

I remember one night a guy at a gas station on Peoria Street had cleaned the garage floor with gasoline. The place was closed, and he had the doors down because it was cold outside.

He put a cigarette in his mouth, lit a Zippo lighter ... and the whole thing went up.

When we pulled up in our car, most of the skin on his arms, chest, and just about everywhere else was coming off. It was a horrible sight. We called for an ambulance, and I got him to lie down. I kept telling him he was going to be all right, but I knew it was a lie. He died a couple of days later.

It wasn't the last time I'd tell a dying man that lie. I was learning very fast that law enforcement can have some really heart-breaking situations.

* * *

I had four great years at college. I lived along the Illinois River for a while, and that meant I could go fishing or hunting whenever I wanted. I left with a BA in sociology, and I also took a lot of psychology courses.

But my real interest was law enforcement. I would have pursued a degree in criminal justice, but I don't think there was a school in the state that offered one back then.

As soon as I got my degree, though, I knew exactly where I was going next—straight back to Tulsa to join the police department.

I signed up for the police academy, which in those days lasted six weeks. And when I got out, the department gave me the assignment I wanted: the patrol division.

CHAPTER 2

My first night out, I rode with Sergeant Leonard Bates (not related to me). It was the evening shift, 2:30 in the afternoon to 10:30 at night, and when I returned the next day, I was just handed the keys and told I didn't need to ride with anybody anymore.

* * *

I rode solo, mostly in West Tulsa and South Tulsa, including Brookside, and I saw everything: murders, rapes, armed robberies, burglaries.

But there was one incident I'll never forget. I was just west of 11th and Denver when I heard a shot. I traveled about fifty yards and came upon a man holding a gun in his hand.

Another man was there, on the ground. It was obvious what had happened.

> **You can't really appreciate what it's like to be a police officer until you've stared point-blank down the barrel of a loaded gun for a few minutes.**

I pulled my gun, approached the gunman, and suggested he might want to consider dropping his weapon.

He wasn't interested. He kept his gun pointed at me, and I fully expected to be shot.

And that's how we stood for about three minutes—an eternity under the circumstances.

It finally dawned on him that shooting me would only make things worse.

He put down his gun, and I handcuffed him and put him in the back of my car.

A HARD CELL

You can't really appreciate what it's like to be a police officer until you've stared point-blank down the barrel of a loaded gun for a few minutes.

* * *

I loved the job, but it didn't last long. In July 1964, about six months after I joined the police department, I married Francey, who had been my girlfriend since high school.

She wasn't very fond of my hours, and, really, who could blame her? I worked evenings for a while, and then I went on the graveyard shift—10:30 at night to 6:30 in the morning.

I was also going to law school three or four nights a week. And I was working part time in a clothing store as a security man, especially during the holidays.

We had a small apartment, and I was gone a lot. We just didn't have a lot of time together for much of anything.

So I quit the police force.

Since I was going to law school at the time, I went to work for a couple of attorneys who had a claims adjustment firm. I handled some liability claims, a few property claims, and so forth—but I really didn't like it.

I might be dealing with people whose kid had been in a car wreck, and maybe somebody had died. My job was to decide what everything was worth, and I'd have to go out and talk to the families. I just never felt good about it, especially if there were kids involved.

And then I got a call from the FBI.

I had taken the FBI test, and the bureau called and asked me to take a physical. After that, an agent and his wife were scheduled to visit Francey and me.

CHAPTER 2

The FBI! I was excited, to say the least. I passed the physical, and then, as promised, the bureau dispatched a couple to speak with us.

I hope for their sake that Mr. and Mrs. FBI did not become job recruiters after they left the bureau. As soon as we met, they proceeded to tell Francey that being an FBI agent's wife would be the most horrible life imaginable. The husband told her I'd end up going to Detroit, Chicago, New York … places that sounded very unappealing to Francey, who had no desire to leave Oklahoma.

My FBI career ended before it even began.

* * *

Not long after that, I got a phone call from the chief of police in Evanston, Illinois, asking if I would be interested in working there.

I said, "Well, what would I be doing?"

He said, "Well, come up and see me."

By this time, Francey was pregnant, but we went anyway.

The first thing we discovered was that it can get very, very cold in Chicago.

We had dinner with the police chief and his wife, and the next day I went to the police station in Evanston. The chief said, "Look, if you will come up here and work with us for thirty-six months, we'll get you into Northwestern University's law school."

That was very enticing. There was no way I could afford to pay for that myself.

"And once you graduate," the chief continued, "you'll give us thirty-six months on contract, doing whatever we need you to do around here as a cop and as an attorney."

It was a wonderful opportunity.

But I told them, sorry, no.

Bob and Francey Bates belonged in Oklahoma.

* * *

And that's how I ended up in the insurance business. We returned home, and I went to work for Rich and Cartmill, a long-established agency in Tulsa. Some great people worked there, including Dick Teubner, who became my mentor.

The first year can be very rough for an insurance salesman, especially one in his early twenties. People look at you and say, "Come back and see me in a couple of years—if you're still in the business."

But I gotta eat now—not in a couple of years!

Teubner gave me advice throughout that first year, and I'm grateful to this day for everything he did. He was my friend then, and he's my friend now. We still talk.

Not unexpectedly, things went very slowly for the first twelve months. But then they began to pick up, and I started to make really good money. And I picked up some excellent customers whom I kept for thirty, forty years.

I stayed with Rich and Cartmill for about eleven years, until I left to start a company of my own. I took my friend Dave Campbell with me. He and I had the same interests. We fished all the time, every week right through the winter.

We started out with two women working for us in a high-rise building in South Tulsa. One, named Debbie Morris, would work with me for the remainder of my insurance career.

Then I brought in three or four other guys to work with us, and we needed more space. So we moved to another building.

We kept growing and needed more space again. This time, in partnership with another fellow, we put up our own building. We split the space in half.

But before long, we outgrew that too, and we moved into a Tulsa high-rise, taking up most of the floor there.

Then we moved again, to the top of another high-rise. But then a major oil company moved in and took most of the building—and it wanted our space. So we moved one last time, to another space that was pretty much the same size.

I ended up running Robert Bates Insurance for forty years. At various times, our agency insured eighteen drilling rigs in Afghanistan. We insured a condom factory in India. I was a correspondent at Lloyds of London. I found the business fascinating.

I had more than fifty employees, including seventeen salespeople, when I finally sold the agency.

* * *

Time is nobody's friend. It takes its inevitable toll in every imaginable way. It took a toll on my marriage to Francey, and we divorced in 1985. It took a toll on my body; I underwent surgery for prostate cancer in 1996.

But clouds have silver linings. Francey and I produced two wonderful daughters, Leslie and Kathy. I've been a cancer survivor for twenty-four years.

And three years after my divorce, I married Charlotte. We've been together for twenty-nine years.

I've had other successes too. I was on the board of Arvest Bank for fifteen years. I became an instrument-rated pilot. I became a pretty good golfer too. I'll never play Augusta, though.

And I did very well in my insurance business—and I tried very hard to do something positive with my success. I used my money and my name to help make my hometown a better place to live.

* * *

There are four hundred thousand people in Tulsa, and, like most US cities, it has big drug problems. But Tulsa is *my* city, and that makes its problems *my* problems.

In the early 2000s, the drug of choice was methamphetamine, and I wanted to help push it out of our city.

One of my clients at Robert Bates Insurance was Stanley Glanz, the sheriff of Tulsa County. I'd been acquainted with him since my time with the Tulsa Police Department, and now I was handling his home and car insurance.

Stanley would come by my office now and then, and we would talk about all the problems in the North Tulsa community—about drugs and how kids were getting their hands on guns and shooting each other—and one day he said to me, "You have a police background. Why don't you come down and become a reserve deputy?"

"I don't know," I said. "I'm too old."

"No, you're not," he said. "You can do it. You're physically OK, as far as I know."

We discussed it a few more times, and the more we talked about it, the more interested I got. Finally, I told him, "Well, I'll volunteer for a few weeks. Let me see what things are like and I'll decide if I want to go further."

I went over to the sheriff's department, and I did some volunteer work for a few weeks in the jail investigations division. Then I went back and said I wanted to get involved with the Narcotics Task Force, which included eight or nine deputies and had two FBI agents and a part-time ATF agent working with it.

I liked almost all the guys, and I trained with them for at least a year.

Just like that, I was back in law enforcement.

And this time, my wife was on board.

CHAPTER 2

* * *

There were more than one hundred sheriff's reserves in Tulsa County, and a lot of them were older and not very active. They'd come out and do the county fair, riding in golf carts, looking for lost kids, stuff like that.

But a reserve deputy can do all the things a regular sheriff's deputy can do in Oklahoma, and I wasn't signing up to ride in a golf cart. I had a background in law enforcement, and I wanted to be an active team member.

Most sheriff's deputies in the state get certified by CLEET—the Council on Law Enforcement Education and Training—whose mission is "to provide the citizens of Oklahoma with peace officers who are trained to be professional, ethical, conscientious, sensitive to needs of the public, knowledgeable and competent …"

* * *

I gave much more than just my time. I was with the Narcotics Task Force for about seven years, and it had very inadequate equipment. My insurance business had made me wealthy, and I had the means and the desire to help. I donated six figures' worth of equipment, including five cars.

I spent eight thousand dollars to buy a cellphone analysis system I'd seen at the FBI. Using it, they could plug in a phone and see emails and text messages and listen to calls. Our conviction rate went up into the ninety-something percentile after I bought that.

I raised quite a lot of money in the business community from some very well-known names in Tulsa. They'd step up and say, "What can we do to help this thing?"

I bought the department a drug-sniffing dog.

When the sheriff's office wanted to buy a three-shot Taser, I went to the factory in Arizona and shelled out sixteen hundred dollars to buy one. I brought it back, tested it, messed with it, and told the sheriff's office it would be a big mistake to get one for the jail. It was just too complicated. When you're under stress and pressure, you can't start punching in numbers on the back of your weapon. I told the sheriff's office not to buy the thing, and it didn't.

> **I did everything I could to clean up Tulsa and make it a better place for the people who live there—because the city was my home.**

I went to St. Paul, Minnesota, to get certification in how to tear down a meth lab, and I spent a week in Dallas at a homicide school.

I did a lot of traveling to become better trained and better educated, and in most cases I paid for everything out of my own pocket. Transportation, accommodations, rental cars … whatever. I wanted to learn how to do things right.

I participated in well over three hundred drug raids, serving as a containment deputy at the scene.

I carried a defibrillator. I had fire department training. I carried bolt cutters, gloves, general hand tools, rapid battery chargers, two crowbars, and two machetes for cutting down marijuana plants.

I did everything I could to clean up Tulsa and make it a better place for the people who live there—because the city was my home.

And that's what I was doing on Thursday, April 2, 2015, when everything I'd been working for crashed and burned.

3

MY PHONE RANG on April Fools' Day, and that's when I made my first mistake: I answered it.

If I could go back in time, I'd let it ring all night.

Sheriff's Deputy Lance Ramsey—the "kingpin" of the Narcotics Task Force, the man who organized at least half of the team's raids—was on the line.

Ramsey was one hell of an undercover agent. He had a way of getting people to like him, and it seemed almost as if suspects wanted him, not someone else, to be the one who handcuffed them when they were arrested.

Ramsey was calling to ask if I could help out the next day, when the task force planned to serve three narcotics warrants.

Sure, I said. I had time. I could come down for a few hours in the morning.

He said the first warrant was for a forty-four-year-old addict who'd been in and out of prison for most of his adult life and had been convicted of numerous felonies, including car theft, robbery, escape from prison, larceny, and knowingly concealing stolen property.

His name was Eric Harris, and his most recent lockup had been for assault and battery on a police officer. He was hurtling down a one-way, dead-end street toward a life sentence, and he had to know that his next arrest might well be his last one.

In the short time he'd been out of jail, Harris had offered to provide Ramsey with stolen cars, drugs, guns—pretty much anything Ramsey said he wanted. He'd sold him crystal meth twice in the past few days, and now Ramsey had arranged to buy drugs and a gun from him. This time it would result in Harris's arrest.

Harris wanted to meet at his home, but Ramsey didn't want to be alone with Harris, who was considered armed and dangerous. Ramsey insisted on an open place where deputies could rush to assist him if he was in trouble.

They agreed to meet in a dollar store parking lot. Ramsey would arrive in a beat-up, old pickup truck, and Harris would meet him there, hop in, and sell him the drugs and a gun.

What Harris didn't know was that a few undercover deputies in unmarked cars would be there too.

* * *

This all sounded pretty routine to me: Ramsey would buy the goods, signal the team that the deal had gone down, show his badge, and inform Harris that he was under arrest. The deputies, with guns drawn, would run toward the truck, open the door, read him his Miranda rights, put him in handcuffs—and shove him into the back seat of my car.

If Harris wasn't inclined to get out on his own, they'd drag him out, put him on the ground, read him his Miranda rights, slap on the handcuffs—and escort him into the back seat of my car.

CHAPTER 3

In the worst-case scenario, I thought, Harris might bolt from the truck or resist arrest, and they'd have to tase him in the parking lot. Then they'd read him his Miranda rights, put him in handcuffs, and escort him into the back seat of my car.

Those were the options, and he'd get to choose. But one way or another, on April 2, 2015, Eric Harris would wind up in the back seat of my car.

I'd have the honor of "taking him to the office."

That's what we called the jail.

* * *

I was accustomed to being the designated chauffeur for these busts. Most of the deputies don't like going to the Tulsa jail. It's very big and has several floors, and the inmates it takes in for booking come not only from Tulsa County but from surrounding counties that lack jails or food or facilities to take care of them.

The state police and the Oklahoma Highway Patrol bring their inmates there too, so it's not unusual to arrive at the jail to book a suspect—only to find yourself waiting for an hour and a half, or more, behind ten arrests in front of you.

That's why the other deputies always were more than happy to have me take their suspects to the office. I did the jobs they didn't want to do—and that was fine with me. I'd done it several hundred times, and it had become very routine.

I was prepared to transport Harris to the office for interviews and to do the paperwork.

Then I'd take him to jail, book him, fingerprint him, and turn him over to the jail crew.

* * *

I woke up at around 6:30 the next morning and got dressed for the job. I couldn't find my Glock—it was either locked up in the safe or in a drawer somewhere—so I picked up a Smith & Wesson .38 and stuck it in the holster at my hip.

Then I left my house in South Tulsa and drove downtown to the sheriff's office, in the Faulkner Building.

We gathered at the Narcotics Task Force office, and Ramsey briefed us all about Harris. Some of the guys thought they'd seen him before, that he was a member of the Crips gang.

Ramsey said Harris had beaten up a cop in Oklahoma City, had been involved in armed robbery, and had been in the correction system for twenty-two years—exactly half his life.

Now he was out of prison again and back at work in the drug and stolen property business. It was the only job he'd ever held, and our job was to shut him down.

* * *

A little after 8:00 a.m., we left the Faulkner Building in about eight cars and drove roughly ten miles to the neighborhood where Ramsey and Harris had agreed to meet. I was assigned to block intersections when necessary—even if there was a red light—so the entire convoy could go through.

Ramsey drove his truck to the parking lot outside the Dollar Store. A few deputies driving unmarked cars went there too. Four of us, in three marked cars, took up positions several blocks away at a gas station. We would hang back until we got word from Ramsey that the deal had gone down.

One of the deputies parked alongside me was a dog handler, and the other two—a man and a woman—were working together. We sat

CHAPTER 3

there, and I spoke with them a couple of times through the window. I was the only reserve deputy in the group.

* * *

Ramsey was wearing a concealed mic, so we could hear him and Harris talking in the truck. It was a typical conversation—Do you need a car? More drugs? Another gun? What do you need?—until something spooked Harris.

Maybe he spotted the undercover cops and smelled a rat. Or maybe something else just didn't look right. Whatever it was, Harris figured out that Ramsey was no deadbeat looking to buy some meth and a gun.

He also knew that if he went to prison again, he probably wouldn't come out on his feet. The next time he left prison, it would be in his coffin.

So he bolted. He opened the door and was gone in seconds.

Go! Go! Go!

Ramsey shouted those words over the radio, and the four of us who had held back raced from the gas station to the Dollar Store.

He's out and running!

Harris took off down Harvard Avenue, with two deputies in pursuit.

I hit my lights and followed the two other marked cars down the street. He was on the run, and all I could think was …

He's presumed to be armed and dangerous. Does Harris still have his gun? Or did Ramsey have it? And even if Ramsey has it, could Harris have another?

I was halfway down the street, still driving my car, when I caught up to one of the others. And suddenly, there was Harris, running right past my passenger door. And I thought …

What in the world is this guy doing?

With a pepper ball gun in my left hand, my revolver at my hip, and a Taser X26 strapped to my chest, I jumped out of my car and joined the chase. I pulled out my revolver while I was running, because Harris was holding his side, and I thought he must have another gun. (In law enforcement, you always assume that when a suspect has a gun, he or she probably has another. It's called one plus one.)

Two deputies were running next to me, and there were several others behind me. Two of them were young and fast, and they caught up to Harris, jumped him, and put him down.

I put my revolver back in its holster.

I caught up to the others, stood over Harris's back, and put my knee on his spine. The deputies wanted to put him in handcuffs, but he had his arm pinned beneath him, and he was doing everything he could to keep it there. He wasn't letting them pull it free.

And the more he resisted, the more I thought he had a gun in that concealed hand and that at some point he would pull it out and start shooting.

I was thinking ...

There's going to be another shooting. If he's got a gun, it's going to come out here directly, and he's going to start shooting.

Our guys are going to get shot. These guys are fairly young, and oh my God he's going to kill them.

I thought it would be very appropriate to zap him with my Taser before that happened.

* * *

There's a clinical term for what came next. Psychologists call it slip and capture. It's when people in high-stress situations mistakenly do one thing when they intend to do another.

CHAPTER 3

I was above Harris, with my pepper gun in my left hand, my revolver in the holster on my right hip, and my Taser strapped to my chest.

I yelled, "Taser! Taser! Taser!" and I saw an opening on his right shoulder.

I reached for the Taser with my right hand …

And I pulled my revolver. I shot him in the shoulder.

Only then did I find out that he had nothing in his hand. He was just being difficult.

* * *

As luck would have it, a fire truck was passing by at that exact moment, and it had EMTs on board. They stopped, got out, and came right over. Somebody called for an ambulance, and it arrived in minutes.

Harris was on the ground.

I asked him two or three times, "What are you on?"

Another guy said, "Tell us what you're taking. The ambulance people are here. They need to know what you're on."

Harris told us more than twice that he was loaded up on PCP, but that didn't sound right to me. Guys who are on PCP have superhuman strength. They're like the Incredible Hulk. They can pick up a guy who weighs two hundred pounds and toss him over a fence.

Harris wasn't behaving that way.

It turned out that what he had in his system was a large, potentially lethal, dose of meth. He'd just run about a quarter of a mile, and his heart had to be racing on overdrive.

* * *

They put Harris into the ambulance and rushed him to the hospital, where he died.

They put me into Sgt. Dave Roberts's car and had me wait until an investigator from the internal affairs department came to take me downtown for questioning. There was nothing unusual about that; they do it whenever a law enforcer shoots someone.

What was unusual was what I found out much later—that one of the deputies who had been sitting with me at the gas station had recorded everything on a video camera he had hidden in his sunglasses.

He'd recorded the chase. He'd recorded the takedown. He'd recorded the shooting. And he'd recorded me saying, "I shot him. I'm sorry."

Those words will follow me everywhere I go, forever.

4

I THINK THE BRAIN has a way of shutting down and protecting you at times like this, because I can't remember much of what happened the rest of the day. Looking back on it now, I think I was in shock. All I remember for sure is that I felt terrible.

A lifelong criminal with a lengthy arrest record—a man who had spent most of his adult life in prison—fled from an arresting officer and continued to resist arrest, even when he had been caught and wrestled to the ground. I thought he was reaching for a concealed gun, and I reached for my Taser so I could subdue him. I grabbed my revolver by mistake, and I shot him.

It had all been in the line of duty, but still … a man had been shot and was being rushed to the hospital—and I was the one who had shot him. It was a horrible feeling.

I remember Sgt. Roberts coming over to me, taking me by the arm, and saying, "Come over here and sit in my truck."

I remember the major on the scene calling the district attorney's office and asking them to send their two investigators to the scene, and I remember that they both refused to come.

And I remember thinking, "Why? Why would they not come here?" And to this day, I still don't know why. They just wouldn't.

I know I called Charlotte, but I can't remember exactly when.

* * *

CHARLOTTE: *Bob called me right after the shooting, and he said, "I just shot somebody." And he said, "I don't think he is going to live." And I said, "OK, what happened?" And he said, "Well, we were on the drug bust, and I accidentally shot him. I thought I had my Taser out."*

And he said, "They are working on him right now. EMSA is here, and they're working on him, but I don't think he's going to live."

And I said, "OK … Are you OK?"

He said, "Yeah, I'm OK. But, you know, I'm worried about this guy. Let me call you back. I'm going to go over there and see if I can help with anything."

That was our conversation. It was right after he accidentally shot Eric.

* * *

I remember they called the department's internal affairs division and had one of the deputies come out to take me back to the sheriff's office.

I don't remember riding downtown, but I'm sure we didn't discuss anything. The normal procedure in a situation like this is that they don't talk to you seriously about the incident for at least forty-eight hours.

But I do remember being in Meredith Baker's office—she was the legal counsel for the sheriff's office—and that both the sheriff, Stanley Glanz, and the undersheriff, Tim Albin, showed up after a while.

And I remember Glanz telling me, "We'll pick up all the bills. Whatever happens legally, we'll take it from there."

CHAPTER 4

I'm not sure I really believed him, but I remember that it made me feel a little better. I suppose I figured I was going to get sued.

Beyond that, Glanz and I hardly talked about what had happened. He gave me a couple of days.

I also remember that at some point, Major Tom Huckeby came into Baker's office. I looked at him and said, "OK, what's the deal?"

"Ten-seven," he said.

Ten-seven means out of service. Dead. Eric Harris didn't make it.

* * *

I was there for less than an hour. The sheriff's office team didn't want to have much of a conversation with me—it's just not the way things are done—so it wasn't long before they said I could leave.

I got into my car, but I didn't go straight home. I was feeling miserable, and I was still downtown, so I stopped at a Catholic church to speak with a priest. I'm not even Catholic; it just felt like something I should do.

But the door was locked, so I got back into my car and finally went home.

And after that, I don't remember anything. Whatever went on in my house when I got there, I don't remember it. But I felt secure that things would be all right, because I'd been assured by the sheriff, the undersheriff, the major, and everybody around me that everyone knew the shooting had been an accident.

I would have to live with the emotional fallout, but I would live with it as a free man. Everyone was telling me there was no way I would be charged with a crime.

* * *

A couple of days later, I got a call from Scott Wood, a lawyer who did a lot of defense work for the Tulsa Police Department and the sheriff's office. He told me that a videotape had surfaced, and he wanted me to come down and see it.

And that was when I discovered that one of the deputies had recorded everything through a camera attached to his sunglasses.

* * *

CHARLOTTE: *Bob and I went to Wood's office, and we viewed the tape over and over and over again. Bob had said all along, "I pulled my Taser, and I yelled, 'Taser! Taser! Taser!'"—which is what you are supposed to do as a law officer before you fire the Taser so the other officers know to get back.*

We viewed this tape over and over and over again, and, thank God, you hear Bob shouting "Taser! Taser! Taser!" and then you hear the bang, and he drops the gun.

The gun actually kind of flew out of his hand, because he was not expecting that recoil. He thought it was the Taser.

So the videotape was very clear, and we thought, well, this proves it was an accident. And I recall us thinking everything was going to be OK.

* * *

It wasn't long before we began to think otherwise. Everything was *not* OK.

Tulsa Sheriff's Department detectives called me back a couple of days later—Scott Wood was with me—and took me into a private room. They were working on their reports in the detective division, and they wanted to ask me some questions about what had happened.

I gave them the abridged version:

I feared for my life, Harris was resisting, he wouldn't pull his hand out from underneath him, we had just bought a gun from him, I was concerned about a "one plus one," I reached for my Taser, I grabbed my gun by mistake, and I accidentally shot him.

CHAPTER 4

And then they read me my Miranda rights.

I had the right to remain silent. Anything I said could and would be used against me in a court of law. I had the right to an attorney. If I couldn't afford an attorney, one would be appointed for me.

I can recite those words in my sleep—I've read them to countless suspects over the years. But I never thought someone would ever read them to me.

Everyone had been telling me there was no way I would be charged … everyone said they knew it was an accident … and here I was, being read my Miranda rights.

Up until this point, all I'd felt was terrible. Now, for the first time, I felt very uncomfortable.

* * *

The Tulsa County district attorney, Steve Kunzweiler, had been in office for about four months when the incident occurred, and now, suddenly, he was under a lot of pressure.

Eric Harris, a black man, was dead. Robert Bates, the reserve deputy who had shot him, was white. And the Black Lives Matter movement and the media were paying very close attention.

It was just three years after a white neighborhood watch patrolman killed Trayvon Martin, an unarmed black teenager, in Sanford, Florida; nine months after a white police officer in New York City put an unarmed black man, Eric Garner, in an illegal—and deadly—chokehold; eight months after a white police officer in Ferguson, Missouri, shot Michael Brown, an unarmed black man, to death, an incident that ignited rioting and protests for weeks; five months after a police officer shot and killed Tamir Rice, a twelve-year-old boy, in Cleveland.

Black Lives Matter had grown into a nationwide cause, and now it had a new grievance: the shooting of Eric Harris in Tulsa, Oklahoma. And Kunzweiler was under considerable pressure to find a responsible party and make him pay.

And that would be me. Black Lives Matter and We the People Oklahoma were demonstrating, the press was milking the story for all the headlines it was worth, and I was caught in the crosshairs.

On the morning after the shooting, I got a call from a reporter at the *Tulsa World*. The next day, the newspaper published a story with the headline "Reserve Deputy Who Shot, Killed Man Thought He Drew His Taser, Release Says."[1]

"Bates confirmed in a phone interview with a *Tulsa World* reporter Friday that he shot and killed Eric Courtney Harris the previous day," the story said.

"'It was me,' Bates said during the interview. 'My attorney has advised me not to comment. As much as I would like to, I can't.'"

* * *

I couldn't comment, but it seemed like everyone else could.

Three days later, the *Tulsa World* published a story under the headline "Sheriff's Office: Reserve Deputy Who Fired Fatal Shot Was Among 'Lots Of' Wealthy Donors in Reserve Program." The story noted that I had "donated thousands of dollars' worth of items to the Sheriff's Office since becoming a reserve deputy in 2008."[2]

A spokeswoman for the sheriff's office was quoted in the story as saying that "There are lots of wealthy people in the reserve program … Many of them make donations of items. That's not unusual at all." She added that I was an unpaid "advanced reserve" who could "do anything a full-time deputy can do."

Nonetheless, a storyline was being developed:

CHAPTER 4

Robert Bates was a wealthy old man involved in "pay for play." He donated equipment and cars to the sheriff's department, and in exchange, they let him play sheriff's deputy.

It was BS, and it was offensive. But on the advice of my lawyer, I couldn't defend myself.

* * *

The pay-for-play story was gathering steam. Within a week, it was making headlines throughout the country—in major newspapers and news magazines, on the radio, on network and cable TV, and on the internet. The shooting of Eric Harris was national news, and the man who shot him was rapidly becoming a national pariah.

* * *

CHARLOTTE: *All they wrote was it was pay-for-play, rich white insurance executive kills unarmed black man.*

It was all over the television. It was all over the news. It was all over everything. But that's just not the way it was. Bob was in shock and absolutely devastated because Eric Harris lost his life.

It was bothering him so much. He couldn't sleep. It was haunting him, and at some point he went to see a priest in his old neighborhood and spent three hours talking with him. It was tearing him up inside.

I remember right after Bob called me, right after he shot Eric, I called my sister. She lives right down the street, and I was very upset, and she came down to my house. I started crying, and I said, "Bob accidentally shot this man, and I think he is going to die."

She said, "Oh my God, what happened?" And I told her what I knew, and she tried to calm me down. She said, "It's going to be OK, he's an officer of the law, he was on duty, it was an accident." And then my employees, people who work for me … everyone was saying he's a policeman, he was doing his job.

* * *

The Miranda rights were a wake-up call. Once they read them to me, I knew it was time to stop listening to all the people who were telling me everything would be OK. I needed a lawyer. A good one.

> **I needed a lawyer. A good one.**

I started spending time with Clark Brewster and his son, Corbin, of Brewster & DeAngelis, one of the most respected criminal defense law firms in Oklahoma. They began planning a strategy for me if Kunzweiler decided to press charges.

Clark was not the least bit concerned. He told me, "Well, this is going to be like shooting fish in a rain barrel. This will never come to anything, it will never amount to anything. You will be released at trial, and that will be it."

* * *

About a week after the shooting, Undersheriff Albin called me—or maybe I called him—and he told me Kunzweiler had charged me with a felony.

I called Clark Brewster, and he already knew. He said he was arranging for us to go to court, where I would be formally arrested and fingerprinted, and he had called the bondsman who would post my bail.

On April 13, eleven days after the shooting, Charlotte and I got up early. I dressed in a suit, and we went to Clark's office.

He drove us down, and it was all very quick. I was formally charged with second-degree manslaughter involving culpable negligence. I was fingerprinted. We waived a preliminary trial. I pleaded not guilty. The bondsman posted my $25,000 bail, and I was on my way home before I knew it.

CHAPTER 4

* * *

In a statement, Kunzweiler explained the charges:

"Oklahoma law defines culpable negligence as 'the omission to do something which a reasonably careful person would do, or the lack of the usual ordinary care and caution in the performance of an act usually and ordinarily exercised by a person under similar circumstances and conditions.'

"The defendant is presumed to be innocent under the law, but we will be prepared to present evidence at future court hearings."

He said I was presumed to be innocent, but you could have fooled me.

Clark and Charlotte weren't the only ones who escorted me to the courthouse. A lot of others tagged along, and it was very clear that they didn't presume me to be innocent.

There were probably thirty or forty media people with cameras outside the front door of the courthouse when I went inside. And they were there when I came back out.

* * *

CHARLOTTE: *The minute Bob got out of his car, those cameras were on top of him. They shoved them in his face. It was a mob, and he could barely walk. It was like he was the president of the United States.*

They followed him as far as they could before a court officer stopped them. It was horrible.

* * *

I was free on bond—but I was very concerned. I looked at the penalties, and they ranged anywhere from a year in the county jail to four years in the state penitentiary.

And I knew for sure that there were a lot of people who wanted the next uniform I wore to be an orange jumpsuit. In just eleven days, I had gone from everyone telling me everything would be OK to feeling like the whole world wanted me behind bars.

* * *

CHARLOTTE: *It was always reported how bad Bob was and how the sheriff's department was not good. They had it on the front page of the newspaper immediately.*

That is all the public read for a whole year: how bad Bob Bates was.

Looking back, we should have just said, "Put the handcuffs on him and he'll do his time," because the press found him guilty before the trial. The press absolutely crucified him.

5

"THE DEFENDANT IS presumed to be innocent under the law."

That's what District Attorney Steve Kunzweiler said. That's what they always say.

But it sure didn't feel that way to me.

In the year and a week between April 13, 2015, when I was formally charged with manslaughter, and April 20, 2016, when my trial began, I was portrayed in the press as a reckless, dangerous, feeble, doddering old man who never should have been allowed anywhere near a car or a gun.

So never mind what the DA said. I was presumed to be guilty. I would be tried and convicted in the media before I ever set foot in a courtroom.

On April 11, the *Tulsa World* published a cartoon that targeted not only me but the entire sheriff's department. It showed a vending machine filled with uniforms. On the top of the machine were the words, "So You Want to Be a Tulsa County Reserve Deputy." On the side was a money slot with the words "Donate Here … Large Bills Only."

The cartoon's message was crystal clear. A storyline—"Wealthy Bob Bates Paid to Dress Up and Play Sheriff, and He Shot an Unarmed Black Man to Death"—was being created. It would sell newspapers, it would lure TV viewers, and it would exact a toll on me, my family, the sheriff's department, and the general public long before I had my day in court.

* * *

Throughout the month, the *Tulsa World* was relentless in its pursuit of "justice," offering multiple stories every day about the shooting, my background, and my work for the sheriff's department. These are just some that appeared in a single week:

April 12: "Tulsa World Editorial: Time for a Thorough Review of Tulsa County Reserve Deputy Program"[3]

April 14: "Reserve Deputy Charged with Manslaughter; Family of Man Killed Says Response Mishandled"[4]

April 15: "Protest Rally Draws Crowd, Ends at Tulsa County Sheriff's Doorstep"[5]

April 16: "Sources: Supervisors Told to Falsify Reserve Deputy's Training Records; Department Announces Internal Review"[6]

April 18: "Friday Night Protest March Seeks Firings of Deputies, Targets Tulsa County Sheriff, Too"[7]

April 18: "Tulsa County Reserve Deputy Apologizes to Slain Man's Family, Criticizes Reports of Impropriety"[8]

All of that in a single week. Nowhere did anyone suggest that I might actually be innocent.

* * *

On April 13, hours after I was charged, Eric Harris's family held a press conference to condemn the sheriff's office and demand a public apology.

"I don't think this has anything to do with race," Harris's brother, Andre, said.[9]

"This is simply evil. We're going to expose it. We're going to pull the mask off the evil. We're going to shine a light on the darkness. We're going to change, here, in our community."

Just one day earlier, Harris's family issued a statement[10] condemning the sheriff's investigation of the shooting. Addressing the shooting itself, the family said:

> [W]e still have many concerns and unanswered questions. Bob Bates, the man who shot Eric in the back at close range with his own personal firearm, is a 73-year-old reserve deputy. He is a wealthy man who has contributed vehicles, equipment and money to TCSO [Tulsa County Sheriff's Office]. Mr. Bates has a close personal relationship with Sheriff Glanz and Undersheriff Tim Albin. Mr. Bates contributed thousands to Sheriff Glanz's campaign. TCSO has every reason to want to protect Bob Bates. They claim that the shooting was a justifiable mistake. They claim that Bob Bates did not violate any policy or law because he believed that he was discharging his taser when he shot Eric in the back with his own personal .38 snub nose pistol. Is this a reasonable explanation? We do not believe that it is reasonable for a man who claims to have all the necessary training to mistake a pistol for a taser. We do not believe it is reasonable for a 73-year-old insurance executive to be involved in a dangerous undercover sting operation. We do not believe it is reasonable for Bob Bates to be carrying a gun that was not issued by TCSO. We do not believe it is reasonable—or

responsible—for TCSO to accept gifts from a wealthy citizen who wants to be [a] "pay to play" cop.

On April 16, the *Tulsa World* published a story headlined "Sources: Supervisors Told to Falsify Reserve Deputy's Training Records; Department Announces Internal Review."[11] According to the report, "Supervisors at the Tulsa County Sheriff's Office were ordered to falsify a reserve deputy's training records, giving him credit for field training he never took and firearms certifications he should not have received, sources told the *Tulsa World*.

"At least three of reserve deputy Robert Bates' supervisors were transferred after refusing to sign off on his state-required training, multiple sources speaking on condition of anonymity told the *World*." This was a complete lie. All three were promoted—one to sergeant and two to captain.

Those "multiple sources" were criticizing not just me but the entire sheriff's department.

The newspaper did not identify them. All I know is that they were lying.

* * *

The drumbeat of negative stories was framing public opinion, but on the advice of my attorney, I stayed quiet—with one exception:

I agreed to be interviewed—with Charlotte, my daughters, and Clark Brewster at my side—by Matt Lauer on the *Today* show.[12]

The interview took place on April 17, the same day the *Tulsa World* published a nineteen-photo gallery with the headline "Hundreds March for Justice in Downtown Tulsa"[13] and another story headlined "Sheriff's Spokesman: Parts of Reserve Deputy's Training Requirements Might Have Been Waived."[14] Again, this was not true. My records were given to me after my release from prison. The Sherriff's Office stated that my records may have accidentally been shredded.

Over a satellite connection, Lauer showed the now-infamous video recording of the shooting, and he asked me to describe what had happened. Later in the interview, he asked me to stand and show him where I held my Taser and my gun.

And then he asked me about the press coverage:

"Mr. Bates," he said, "in the wake of this incident, you have been portrayed as a wealthy and generous supporter of the sheriff's department and a close friend of the sheriff, who has been rewarded for your financial support with the opportunity—and this is what's out there—to play cop and carry a gun. Is that a fair characterization?"

My reply was short and simple:

"That is unbelievably unfair," I told him.

Not that it mattered.

* * *

For a while, it seemed like everyone wanted to get involved. The Harris family's lawyer, Daniel Smolen, told the press that "America is going to see what happens after a bad shooting takes place, when a law enforcement agency refuses to step up to the plate."[15]

The American Civil Liberties Union of Oklahoma released a statement calling for an end to "Buy a Badge" programs—or volunteer units—in law enforcement.

And then came the biggest blow of all.

On April 22, the *CBS Evening News* broadcast a report[16] that shocked not only me and my family but the entire Tulsa community. It was accompanied by a story on the network's website with the headline **"Deputy Who Fired Gun Instead of Taser Was Investigated in 2009"**:

TULSA, Okla.—CBS News has learned that a 2009 investigation by the Tulsa Sheriff's Office concluded that there were concerns over Robert Bates' behavior in the field ...

[T]he Tulsa Sheriff's Office launched an internal investigation to find out if Bates received special treatment during training and while working as a reserve deputy. They also investigated whether supervisors pressured training officers on Bates' behalf.

The investigation concluded Bates' training was questionable and that he was given preferential treatment ...

A spokesman for the Tulsa Sheriff acknowledged that some type of internal review was conducted, but that there was no further action taken. Sheriff Stanley Glanz said this week he believes Bates received his required training.

* * *

I'd never heard of any such report, and neither, it seemed, had the sheriff's office. As for the *Tulsa World*, it got scooped in its own backyard and had to scramble to catch up with CBS.

The next day, the newspaper reported:

When asked about the allegations in the CBS report, Tulsa County Sheriff's Maj. Shannon Clark said he had learned that a past under-sheriff ordered "some type of internal review" into Bates but that it was never classified as an investigation and that there was "no further action" in the review.

"The Sheriff's Office has no documented record of a report being generated," Clark said.

CHAPTER 5

> *Tulsa County Sheriff Stanley Glanz mentioned a report regarding Bates made by the same undersheriff in a Monday news conference, but he said he believed that report concluded that Bates received "no special treatment."* [17]

I didn't know of this report. The investigation was closed with no additional action taken. There was no truth in the report, and I can prove it with my records.

On April 25, three days after CBS News broke the story, the *Tulsa World* finally got its hands on the six-year-old report and provided a link to it on its website.[18]

I could write another book dedicated solely to refuting just about every single-spaced line in its thirteen pages, but what's the point? I went to prison. It's too late now.

But there are a few things that really do need to be addressed.

According to the report, I did not complete the required 480 field training hours for advanced status as a reserve deputy. That just wasn't true. In fact, I completed even more hours than was required.

It said there was no evidence that I had taken the required written exam. That also wasn't true. I remember it took two or three hours. I returned it when finished to a secretary by the name of Bonnie.

It said there was no evidence that I had undergone the required physical exam. Again, not true. I went to my own doctor, I took the physical, I had a stress test, a hearing test, a vision test—everything required.

Another thing: my biggest critic in the 2009 report was Corporal Warren Crittenden. He said he "felt pressured" to sign off on my training and that he didn't write either of two memos with his name on them that stated I had concluded my training. He said he was given them to initial, and he did so because "he was afraid of trouble like a transfer if he did not."

That's the same Warren Crittenden who was sitting in jail when I shot Eric Harris. He was behind bars, without bail, facing a charge of first-degree murder of a man who was shot to death in a motel room three months earlier. Charges against Crittenden were dismissed in August when he agreed to testify against his three codefendants.

On August 21, 2015, the *Tulsa World* reported:[19]

Two months after Crittenden was charged in the motel slaying, a 2009 Internal Affairs report revealed he supervised some reserve deputy training for Bates, who faces a second-degree manslaughter charge in the April 2 death of Eric Harris. ... In the report, Crittenden said he felt pressured by then-Capt. Tom Huckeby to produce reports showing Bates was trained despite his belief to the contrary, and said many training documents containing his signature were forged.

Tulsa County Sheriff's Office officials previously told the World that Crittenden was a disgruntled former employee and questioned his credibility because at the time he was a murder defendant.

* * *

Many of the "facts" in the 2009 report were flat-out wrong, and my accusers' motives were suspect, but what rankles me most about it is this:

Why, if I was unfit to be a reserve deputy, was I allowed to continue to serve in that role for six more years?

If I was so incompetent, why did the Tulsa County Metro Drug Task Force thank me in a letter "for all that you do and all you have accomplished" and "for a job well done" in 2011?

If I was so incompetent, how did it come to pass that I was named the Reserve Deputy of the Year for "dedicated service to law enforcement and public service to the people of Tulsa County" in 2012?

And, most important, why wasn't I ever told that this investigation had been conducted and that a report had been filed?

If I wasn't wanted, if I was considered unfit and unqualified … why on earth didn't anyone tell me? Why was this report kept hidden from me for six years?

In fact, why was this report kept hidden from just about everyone in the department? Undersheriff Tim Albin said he'd never seen it. Major Tom Huckeby said he'd never seen it.

I became a reserve deputy to help the citizens of Tulsa, my hometown. If I wasn't wanted, I would've walked in and said, "Look, if you guys don't want me around here, I don't have a problem. There are other people in town who could use my help and my money. It doesn't have to be here."

* * *

The drumbeat at the *Tulsa World* never stopped. It just kept getting louder:

April 21: "Two Deputies Reassigned in Wake of Fatal Shooting by Tulsa County Reserve Deputy"[20]

April 23: "Sheriff's Office Confirms Prior Internal Review of Reserve Deputy Robert Bates"[21]

April 24: "Attorneys Demand Tulsa County Sheriff Release Report on 2009 Investigation of Reserve Deputy"[22]

April 25: "Protesters Applaud Possibility of Further Investigation into Tulsa County Sheriff's Office"[23]

April 25: "Internal Investigation Focused on Top Deputies in Sheriff's Office"[24]

April 25: "2009 Internal Memo Details Investigation Critical of Robert Bates' Treatment, Training"[25]

April 26: "Public Scrutiny Over Robert Bates' Conduct, Training Puts Reserve Deputy Program Under Microscope"[26]

April 27: "Reserve Deputy Robert Bates' Age, Place on Violent Crimes Task Force Questioned by Expert"[27]

May 13: "Autopsy: Eric Harris Had Meth, Not PCP, in His System When Shot by Reserve Deputy"[28]

* * *

I shot Eric Harris, and the fallout was immediate. The shooting triggered a chain of events that may never be forgotten in Tulsa:

On May 1, Undersheriff Tim Albin resigned under pressure and began his retirement.

On May 30, the sheriff's spokesman, Shannon Clark, resigned.

On August 1, Major Tom Huckeby, who oversaw the drug task force, resigned.

On July 16, two days after I formally entered my plea of not guilty, Captain Billy McKelvey was demoted.

On September 25, the *Tulsa World* reported:[29]

More than half of Tulsa County Sheriff's Office reserve deputies' files were missing mandatory training hour records and yearly firearms qualification documentation, and nine advanced reserves hadn't met minimum service hour requirements, an internal audit of the files found.

The 13-page records audit report notes that 64 of 112 reserves were missing documentation or hadn't met the requirements in one or more of the years reviewed. The audit, released Thursday by the Sheriff's Office, examined records from 2008 through 2014.

* * *

CHAPTER 5

On October 1, Sheriff Stanley Glanz resigned. After spending twenty-three years with the Tulsa Police Department, he was elected Tulsa County sheriff in 1988, and he was reelected in 1992, 1996, 2000, and 2004. On the day of his resignation, he was indicted on two misdemeanor charges: refusal to perform official duty and willful violation of the law.

On January 13, Acting County Sheriff Rick Weigel and Chief Deputy John Bowman resigned after a heated meeting over the budget for the county jail. The next day, a new acting sheriff, Michelle Robinette, told the *Tulsa World*, "It's going to take time to trust again."

On April 5, Vic Regalado became Tulsa's first newly elected sheriff in more than three decades.

> **I was a pariah not only among the citizens of Tulsa but within the department as well.**

Even before all of this, there was an undercurrent of resentment toward reserve deputies like me in the Tulsa County Sheriff's Department. We were unpaid volunteers, and there were people who clearly thought we were making it easy for the sheriff not to hire more deputies. I heard on several occasions that I was taking a position that somebody else would be paid to fill if I weren't doing it for nothing.

But now things were worse. The sheriff's department was in turmoil, and it all stemmed from the shooting of Eric Harris. Now I was a pariah not only among the citizens of Tulsa but within the department as well.

* * *

The full-press coverage took a personal toll not only on me but on my family, my friends, and my colleagues.

*　*　*

CHARLOTTE: *Shortly after the shooting, I got a call early in the morning from the general manager of my company, Sheila. She said, "Charlotte, we've been broken into."*

She was really scared, so Bob and I went to my office. What we saw was that someone had taken a big concrete boulder and thrown it through my glass back door.

They walked in and ransacked my office. They tore my desk apart and stole money that we hadn't put in the bank yet.

Nothing like this had ever happened to me before—and I've been in business for thirty-four years now. So to have it happen right after the shooting … well, I can't prove anything. But I'm positive it wasn't a coincidence.

*　*　*

One night, Charlotte and I went out for dinner a couple of miles from our house. We were driving home when three dark-skinned guys in an old pickup truck pulled up beside us on my left. They clearly wanted to run us off the road.

I let them stay alongside me, and they were closing the gap between our cars when we came to an intersection. I made a sudden, sharp right turn and hit the gas. I lost them because I had a very powerful car that would go like a bat out of hell.

Another time, we were sitting at a pizza place, and the server came to our table and said, "You've got a guy down there who's videoing you and Charlotte."

I said, "What for?"

She said, "Well, he's talked about how he likes to try to video you, and then he sends it to the *Tulsa World*."

As for my insurance business, I lost count of how many people called and asked my salespeople how they could work for a murderer. I lost a lot of my customers because of the situation and the publicity that it generated.

Guilty until proven otherwise. It was like that all year.

* * *

But not everyone thought I was a wealthy lowlife who wanted to wear a uniform and shoot people. I had supporters too.

* * *

CHARLOTTE: *About two weeks after the shooting—after the break-in and with all the threats of violence—our attorneys said it might be best if we got out of town for a couple of days, or even weeks. So we decided to go to our second home in Florida.*

Bob had a friend whose cousin ran a limousine service, and—because we didn't want anyone to see us leaving or find out where we were going—he offered to pick us up in the middle of the night and drive us to the airport.

The limo driver showed up at five in the morning, and he didn't want to charge us. He shook Bob's hand and said, "I just want you to know that I think this is wrong, what is going on with you."

* * *

There were other times too. Often, when Charlotte and I would go out to dinner, people would want to pay our bill. Some of them would pay it before we were done. Then they would leave, and I wouldn't know who covered my tab.

* * *

Long before the shooting, I decided I wanted to take my whole family—Charlotte, my six grandchildren, my daughters, and their husbands—to the Bahamas. I rented a nice home there, and we were planning to take a family vacation in June.

After I was indicted, I wasn't sure if I could still do this. So when we got back from Florida, I asked my lawyer, "Do you think it's OK? I've put up a ten-thousand-dollar deposit, and it's nonrefundable."

He said, "Well, yeah, that sounds like that would be OK. Let's take it before the judge."

So we took it to the judge, and she said it would be fine.

But the media didn't think it was fine. As soon as they picked up on my request, I became the guy who killed somebody and now was going off on vacation to walk in the sand.

Guilty until proven otherwise, I chose to cancel the trip.

* * *

CHARLOTTE: *One day ... I came home from the office for lunch or something, and Bob was at work. One of my employees came over to bring me something, and all of a sudden there were reporters on my front porch sticking cameras in my door.*

They were looking in my windows, and this young woman who worked for me—she was twenty-one, I think—was scared. She said, "Charlotte, what do we do?" And I said, "Just stay here. I'm going to call my attorney and see if they can get rid of them."

I called him, and he was very nonchalant about it. He was just like, "It's OK, Charlotte." And I said, "No, it's not OK! It's not OK! Our home is being violated, and I'm tired of this."

You get tired of people following you and following Bob and saying horrible things, and it's day after day after day after day. So the attorney called the police, but by the time they got there, the reporters had left.

CHAPTER 5

We were told to put no trespassing signs—big, orange signs—all around our house. Our neighbors were wondering what was going on with the signs, but they were all very supportive.

Another time, Bob and I were at home, and one of my employees called and said, "Where are you?" I said, "I'm at the house with Bob," and she said, "Well, it's all over the television that you and Bob have left the country."

Long story short, I had a bunch of boxes and clothes stacked by my front door for our cleaning lady to bring upstairs and put in the storage area. The press stuck their cameras in our front door, saw the boxes and clothes, and decided we were packing up to leave the country.

The press did that kind of stuff for the entire year.

* * *

Whenever I would show up anywhere—on a scheduled visit to the courthouse or whatever—there would be at least thirty press people there with their cameras flashing. So many people packed the hall when we went to court that it was a fire hazard.

My sentencing hearing was moved to a different courtroom because there were just too many people there. We had national news people, local news people, and all the news trucks outside with their antennas up. It was unbelievable.

* * *

I heard that there was a rumor going around that I got up bright and early on the morning of the shooting and decided I was going to kill a black man that day.

The State Sheriff's Association and Tulsa County named me deputy of the year in 2012, and a lot of things were taken into consideration to get that honor.

All of a sudden, all of that was in the toilet. Everything I'd done for the sheriff's office had been flushed down the drain.

The press was determined to turn me into a criminal, and it succeeded.

* * *

CHARLOTTE: *It was the persecution of Bob Bates, and it was horrible.*

6

CULPABLE NEGLIGENCE.

Two words—all of six syllables—were the keys to my future.

To find me guilty of second-degree manslaughter, a jury of my peers had to determine, unanimously and beyond a reasonable doubt, that I was "culpably negligent" when I shot Eric Harris—and that my "culpable negligence" had resulted in his death.

That's what the judge told the jury at the end of my six-day trial.

If the jury decided that I was not culpably negligent, I'd walk out of court, grab a bite to eat, go home, and sleep comfortably in my bed.

But if the jury decided that I was culpably negligent and that the bullet I fired was the "direct and proximate cause" of Eric Harris's death, I could go to prison for as much as four years.

According to the Oklahoma Uniform Jury Instructions, Criminal 2nd Edition,[30] culpable negligence "refers to the omission to do something which a reasonably careful person would do, or the lack of the usual ordinary care and caution in the performance of an act usually and ordinarily exercised by a person under similar circumstances and conditions ..."

"Not only culpable negligence, but also a direct and proximate causal link between the defendant's conduct and the consequent death, must be established."

Clark Brewster, my defense attorney, was the best in the business, and he kept reassuring me that there was no way I'd be found culpably negligent—that no jury would find me guilty of manslaughter.

But after a year of constant protests and demonstrations, and amid a ceaseless drumbeat of negative publicity from the print, broadcast, cable, and internet media, I felt I had good reason to be concerned.

* * *

But first, we had to find a judge.

District Judge James Caputo had presided over my arraignment after the shooting. He'd been a deputy sheriff in Tulsa County a couple of decades earlier, and he was approved by both my lawyer and the district attorney.

But Caputo did not mention in his judicial disclosure listing that he had been a reserve deputy sheriff in 2006–2008, and that he had an association with Lance Ramsey, the undercover deputy Harris was running from on the day he was shot.

Caputo had partnered with Ramsey in 1993 and 1995, and he'd been Ramsey's divorce lawyer in 2004. The omission was inadvertent—Caputo had no reason to mention those associations in his disclosure form, because he did not know at the time that Ramsey would be a witness at my trial. But six months after he got the case, a potential conflict had arisen.

In separate statements, an advocacy group called We the People Oklahoma and the attorney for the estate of Eric Harris demanded that Caputo recuse himself from the case. On October 29, he did.

CHAPTER 6

"I think once (Caputo) became more fully aware of who certain witnesses were going to be and what the case ultimately would revolve around, I think at that point he realized, 'All right. This is the best decision for our community,'" District Attorney Steve Kunzweiler said.

One down. Next up to the plate, the on-deck batter: District Judge Sharon Holmes, who got the job just hours after Caputo stepped down—and didn't keep it for as long.

The *Tulsa World* conducted a search of campaign finance disclosures and found that Daniel Smolen II, a partner in the Tulsa law firm Smolen & Roytman, had contributed three thousand dollars to the Committee to Elect Sharon Holmes District Judge 2014.[31]

And it just so happened that Smolen & Roytman was representing Eric Harris's estate in a civil suit.

Clark Brewster, my lawyer, pointed out the conflict of interest to Judge Holmes, and on December 7, she met with us in her chambers and told me, "Mr. Bates, you will have a new judge by dark today."

And that's how and why William Musseman, chief judge of the County Court's criminal division, got the case.

His first decision? Delay the trial for two more months. Forget about February; we'll do it in April.

* * *

Or ... maybe not. When April arrived, my lawyers showed up in court toting 2,447 documents related to my case, as well as a 232-page bound volume titled "Criminal History of Eric Harris." More importantly, they also presented a list of witnesses that included two physicians, which led the DA's office to believe that Brewster was planning to dispute the coroner's report and argue that Harris did not die of a gunshot wound.

And if he didn't, then I could not be held responsible for his death.

On April 11, just as the trial was set to begin, the DA's office asked Musseman to delay the trial further to give the prosecutors time to review all the documents my lawyers had submitted. Thankfully, the judge turned them down. I'd waited long enough to have my day in court.

Later that week, the judge made a number of rulings that would serve as ground rules for the trial:

Prosecutors would not be allowed to present evidence that I had successfully drawn and used a Taser prior to Harris's shooting.

My lawyers would not be allowed to present specific evidence and testimony about Harris's criminal history. We were "not here to litigate Mr. Harris," the judge declared.

The controversial 2009 file that had surfaced since the shooting could not be discussed. Prosecutors could bring up opinions on the "adequacy or insufficiency" of my police training only in cross-examination.

Prosecutors would be allowed to show the jurors the video recording of Harris's shooting—including a controversial segment that showed Harris lying on the ground and complaining that he couldn't breathe, while a deputy who was restraining him told him, "Fuck your breath."

My lawyer argued that those words—even though they were spoken by another deputy—might prejudice the jury. The judge disagreed.

* * *

As the trial approached, my lawyers formulated a two-pronged defense. They would argue that:

In a treacherous moment, with reasonable suspicion that Eric Harris was armed and dangerous, I had reached for my Taser and mistakenly grabbed my gun instead. I shot him, but it was an accident. It was a classic case of slip and capture.

There was no disputing that I'd shot Eric Harris, but the bullet wasn't what killed him. Under the influence of cocaine and methamphetamine, and after running a good distance in an effort to escape, Harris, who had heart disease, went into cardiac arrest and died of a heart attack, not a bullet wound. Harris's death, my lawyers would argue, was an unfortunate coincidence.

I believed then—and I believe now—that both arguments were true. I knew, in my heart, that the shooting was an accident. And after speaking with a slew of physicians, I felt confident that the gunshot wound wasn't what killed him.

But try telling that to the *Tulsa World*, which, on the day before my trial began, published a story with the headline "'Slip and Capture' Could Be Key to Robert Bates' Defense, but Expert Calls Concept 'Junk Science.'"[32]

This one still pisses me off.

First of all … *Expert?*

Let's compare experts.

My expert was the Minnesota-based Force Science Institute,[33] "a world-class team of physicians, psychologists, behavioral scientists, attorneys and other leading professionals … dedicated to the unbiased application and further study of 150 years of existing scientific research on a wide range of areas associated with human factors, including the intricacies of human movement, action/reaction times, how the mind works during rapidly unfolding events, decision-making under stress, etc."

The *Tulsa World*'s "expert" was a University of South Carolina law professor who used to be a police officer.

I'm no journalist, but I know this much: newspapers have an aura of authority and respectability in their community. When a newspaper like the *Tulsa World* calls someone an "expert," the reading public believes he's an expert.

But what if he isn't? Who determines who's an "expert"? The *Tulsa World*?

In this case, the newspaper presented no credentials. They just called their guy a "national policing expert."

And what qualified him to be called that? Damned if I know. And damned if the *Tulsa World* bothered to tell its readers.

All I know is that one day before my manslaughter trial began, the number one newspaper in Tulsa, Oklahoma, saw fit to present a single "expert" with unexplained credentials who would expertly reject the basis of my defense. The *Tulsa World* allowed a man who was not a scientist to say with "authority" that my defense "looks to me like a pseudo-scientific way of trying to explain why somebody made a mistake ... I would say it's not a generally accepted theory or set of principles."[34]

So, on one hand, we had the Force Science Institute. On the other, we had a lawyer who used to be a police officer—a man with no science background and no psychology credentials. Or, as the *Tulsa World* would have you believe, an "expert"—one who was perfectly qualified to call my defense "junk science" one day before my trial began.

But that wasn't all. The *Tulsa World* doubled down that same day with another story, this one carrying the headline "Supporters Gather to Remember Eric Harris on Eve of Bates' Manslaughter Trial":[35]

Marq Lewis, We the People Oklahoma leader and community organizer, planned the vigil to remember Harris' life ...

"We just wanted to remind the state that what they're prosecuting is very important. This is a life that was lost," he said ...

Sunday's vigil included a number of speakers, including State Rep. Regina Goodwin, D-Tulsa; State Sen. Kevin Matthews, D-Tulsa; and candidate for state representative Jonathan Townsend, who encouraged attendees to keep moving forward and demanding justice.

After an hour of speakers and two songs, the vigil ended. Attendees raised their white candles—framed by assorted paper cups or cupcake wrappers—and repeated after Lewis: "With love we can conquer anything."

Those were the only two stories the *Tulsa World* published about my case on the day before my trial began. Clearly, my lawyers and I were going up against much more than an eager district attorney.

* * *

On April 18, sixty-five prospective jurors arrived at the Tulsa County Courthouse and were instructed to fill out a thirty-five-question form[36] designed to detect possible conflicts of interest. Among the questions were:

23. Have you read, seen or heard about this case, the alleged facts of this case?

25. Have you talked about this case with anyone, such as friends, family, neighbors, co-workers or overheard others discussing the case?

Two days later, on April 20, exactly 383 days after the shooting of Eric Harris, the *Tulsa World* reported that twelve potential jurors had been excused, and that two—count 'em, two—"had disclosed on the survey that they had followed media coverage of the case," and that "While one acknowledged she could be fair in deciding a verdict, she said she thought the stories have only presented one side and therefore the prosecution would have a 'head start.'"

The shooting of Eric Harris had launched demonstrations and protests for more than a year, the incident and its aftermath had been covered nonstop by Tulsa's largest newspaper and on cable and network news throughout the country ... and only two prospective jurors said they'd been following the media coverage?

Only two? I found that very hard to believe. Any adults in Tulsa County who did not follow media coverage of the case had to have been hiding under a rock for the past year.

With that in mind, it struck me that I might get a fairer trial in another county, so I asked my lawyer about seeking a change of venue.

He told me, "Well, we might get something worse than what we've got here."

I told him, "I don't think it could be any worse."

But I let it go. Clark Brewster was confident that we would win, and one thing everyone in Tulsa knows is that Clark Brewster is one helluva lawyer. He wins.

* * *

On April 21, twelve jurors—all white—were seated to hear my case, and the district attorney and Brewster made their opening statements.

The DA told the jury that I had shouted that I was going to deploy my Taser, but I grabbed my revolver instead. And then I shot Eric Harris, who died later in the day.

My lawyer told the jurors that they would have to decide whether the deputies who chased and caught Harris decided he posed a serious risk—one that would justify a high stress level that could lead me to accidentally pulling the wrong weapon.

He presented pictures of my Taser and my revolver to show that they were very close in weight and had a similar grip and feel.

CHAPTER 6

Weapon confusion, he told the jury, was "the case … This is not a mistake that's unreasonable. It's predictable."

Brewster said medical experts would testify that, according to the autopsy report, Harris had a heart condition and was high on meth when he died—and that those two factors, plus the strain of running from sheriff's deputies, had caused the heart attack that killed him.

I was nervous as hell. But at least, at long last, my trial had begun.

* * *

Charlotte, her sister, Terrie, and I drove about six or seven miles from our home to Clark Brewster's office every morning of the trial. He was very positive; he said this ought to be an easy deal. We'd sit with him and go over everything with him until he said, "OK, it's time to go," and then we'd go with him and some of his associates to the courthouse.

We'd go through a side door, because the front door was covered wall to wall with members of the press. Then we'd go up to the fourth floor, where spectators would be lining the walls. There were cameras everywhere.

The courtroom was too small to hold everybody—I don't think they'd ever had that many people there. They'd installed metal detectors, and they were checking everybody with a wand, because they were worried about violence.

* * *

CHARLOTTE: *You could feel the tension in the courtroom. The reporters were lined up, trying to get in. Some of them got upset because there were only so many seats, and some of them didn't get in because they weren't there on time.*

Bob sat with his lawyers. And during breaks, I just remember him pacing.

During one break, he tried to interact with Eric Harris's brother, Andre.

He said, "I really like your tie."

And Harris just snapped back at him and said, "I really liked my brother."

After that, the lawyers told Bob, "Don't talk to them. Don't talk to anybody. Don't be nice to anybody. Just be there."

* * *

After both sides made their opening statements, the prosecution proceeded to lay out its case against me.

They played the video of the shooting over and over again. Each time, the jurors saw Harris lying on the ground after he was shot. Each time, he could be heard telling the deputies, "I'm losing my breath."

And each time, they'd hear Deputy Sheriff Joseph Byars say "Fuck your breath."

When Byars took the stand, he testified that he'd watched Harris running, and that he kept "dodging vehicles" as he got "further and further" down the road, and that was why he used those inflammatory words.

"My thinking," he said, "was, 'You're the one that ran, and you're going to complain that you can't catch your breath?'"

But they kept playing the tape over and over. And every time, the jury got to hear a deputy sheriff telling a man who would soon be dead, "Fuck your breath."

It created a terrible image of the sheriff's department. And even though I wasn't the one who said it, I was with the sheriff's department. That didn't sit well with anybody.

* * *

The next day, the prosecutors came up with another argument against me.

Deputy Sheriffs Ricardo Vaca and Miranda Munson, who had been sitting in the car next to mine, testified that they'd seen me dozing off behind the wheel as we waited for the call to assist in Harris's arrest.

They said they looked through my window and saw that my eyes were closed and my head was drooped for several minutes.

I still can't believe they said such a thing. Ask anyone who knows me, and they'll tell you I can't sleep on a plane, a train, a bus—not now and not ever. And I damn sure wouldn't be sleeping during a drug raid.

I remember I was looking at my phone and my head was tilted down. One thing is for certain; I was wide awake.

There's more. My windows were deeply tinted, and I had them rolled up. I remember Vaca and Munson asking me a question at one point—or I was asking them a question—and I rolled my windows down. But while those windows were up, there's just no way they could've seen me through them.

When Brewster finally got to cross-examine the deputies, they admitted that they could only "speculate" that I'd been asleep, and they acknowledged that I might have been looking down or closing my eyes for another reason.

But the damage was done. The seed had been planted. The jurors now suspected that I'd been napping.

* * *

CHARLOTTE: *I know Bob, and I know there is no way that Bob Bates would be sleeping. No way, no how. I will take that to my grave.*

* * *

The prosecution was doing all it could to portray me as a trigger-happy, over-the-hill rich guy looking for a good time—literally. At one point, when Deputy Ramsey was on the stand, the DA said I had phoned him the day before the shooting and asked, "Can we have a good time tomorrow?"

Well, that never happened either. I didn't call Ramsey; he called me. And when he called me, he said, "We need some help."

There was nothing unusual about that; Ramsey did that all the time.

When he called me on April 1, the day before the shooting, I told him, "Yeah, I have time in the morning. I'll do it. But I've got to be back by lunch."

And he told me, "OK."

I wish I'd said I had to be back by breakfast.

* * *

Vaca also testified that he didn't hear me shout out that I was going to deploy my Taser and that I came very close to shooting him while he was on top of Harris.

But how could Vaca not hear me? He was the one wearing the glasses with the hidden video recorder, and all you have to do is watch and listen to his own recording.

Watch it, and you'll hear me clearly shouting, "Taser! Taser! Taser!"—three times.

* * *

CHARLOTTE: *I think Vaca just found an opportunity to say, "Yeah, he was sleeping." And "Yeah, I was in fear of my life."*

Bob was trying to save those men. He thought Eric Harris had another gun. And he was fighting, and Vaca was on top of him, and Vaca had a gun. Harris very easily could've grabbed Vaca's gun and just started shooting people.

* * *

The prosecution rested. Now it was Brewster's turn.

The first prong of my defense was "slips and capture."

A little more than a week after the shooting, I got in touch with the man who coined the term: Dr. Bill Lewinski, the executive director of the Force Science Institute. He was a psychology professor specializing in police psychology for more than twenty-eight years at the University of Minnesota, Mankato.

Lewinski defines "slips and capture"[37] as "mistakes that are made when you think you are doing one thing but you actually are doing another, and the result often is directly opposite of what you intended: 'In effect, your intended behavior "slips off" the path you wanted it to go because it is "captured" by a stronger response and sent in a different direction.'"

I was familiar with the concept of slips and capture. I'd read about it in magazines, and I'd done a little research into it. To me, it made sense that people in stressful conditions could mean to do one thing but do another by mistake.

One of the first examples I'd heard of involved a cop in Oakland, California, who shot a man on a commuter train platform when he intended to tase him. Since then, there have been quite a number of cases in the United States and Canada.

It's not that uncommon, really. The problem is that it's hard to believe it can happen—until it happens to you. And it's hard to explain to others—especially when "experts" tell newspapers that it's junk science.

To explain slip and capture to my jury, Brewster reached out to Dr. Charles Morgan, a forensic psychiatrist from Yale University who studies human cognitive error in stressful situations.

Brewster asked Morgan to come to Oklahoma, and he agreed to testify on my behalf.

When Morgan took the stand, he went into great detail about the brain, and he described my mistake as a muscle memory thing.

The *Tulsa World* reported:[38]

Morgan said that in stressful situations, even highly trained individuals can make mistakes due to a surge of adrenaline blocking "reflective" thinking and leaving "reflexive" or "habitual" actions to kick in.

"When stress goes up, nobody gets smarter," Morgan told the court.

Because of that, Morgan confirmed to Bates' attorney Clark Brewster that in situations such as the gun sting in which a possibly armed suspect is attempting to flee, a lack of mistakes would be "unusual."

* * *

The second prong of my defense was that I didn't kill Eric Harris.

Yes, I shot him. Yes, he died a short while later. But no, I didn't kill him. And since I didn't kill him, I could not be guilty of manslaughter.

Dr. Cheryl Niblo, the coroner who performed the autopsy, wrote on her report that Harris died of a bullet wound.

But it came out in testimony that Niblo had not reviewed the hospital record of Harris's death.

"I performed the autopsy, and his injuries were severe enough that I could determine the cause of death on my own," she told the court.

Brewster pulled out the Department of Corrections records about Harris and his twenty-two years in prison, and he pointed out that at the time Niblo performed the autopsy, Harris had both methamphetamine and cocaine in his system.

He asked Niblo if Harris's heart condition, the high levels of meth in his system, and the exertion from running and wrestling with the deputies who caught him might have caused him to go into cardiac arrest.

"Anything is possible," Niblo replied. "But he had trauma."

But not a lot of trauma, said Dr. Mark Brandenburg, an expert in emergency medicine who also testified in my defense. Niblo's conclusion was "absolutely untrue," he told the jury. The bullet, he said, didn't hit any arteries, veins, or the heart, and it only grazed Harris's right lung, which showed no evidence of even a partial collapse.

Harris had "underlying heart disease," Brandenburg testified, along with elevated adrenaline from trying to escape and a "very high level" of methamphetamine in his system.

Harris didn't die from a bullet wound, Brandenburg said. He died of a massive heart attack.

Dr. James Higgins, a well-known cardiologist, was called to the stand, and he seconded what Brandenburg said. The bullet didn't hit the conduction system of Harris's heart, Higgins told the jury, so it had no effect on the organ's electrical function.

He reached the same conclusion as Brandenburg: Harris died of a heart attack.

* * *

I wanted to take the stand, but my lawyers advised me not to. It's not up to defendants to prove themselves innocent. It's up to the prosecutors to prove them guilty. No defense lawyer would ever put his client on the stand unless he considered it absolutely necessary.

In my case, it wasn't. We were confident that our case was solid, compelling, and based on known science. We felt the jury would be persuaded that:

In a classic example of "slips and capture," I had reached for my Taser, grabbed my gun, and shot Harris by accident. It was a lousy mistake but an honest one, committed by an experienced reserve deputy in a perilous, potentially life-or-death moment.

Harris died shortly after he was shot, but he didn't die of a bullet wound. A career criminal who had spent more than two decades in prison, he was a habitual coke and meth abuser who had heart disease and died from a heart attack. That his heart quit on him soon after he was shot was unfortunate, but it was unrelated to his wound. It was just a sad coincidence.

That was my defense, but the testimony on my behalf was technical and complicated. My lawyer had to explain the science of slips and capture, as well as the science about how the heart works. He had to convince the jury that the bullet wound did not cause a sufficient loss of blood, that it did not hit a vein or an artery, and that it did not damage any internal organ.

And all that science was complicated—much more complicated than the emotional argument that a rich, old, doddering white guy paid to put on a uniform and play deputy and that he shot a black man recklessly in the line of duty.

Brewster was talking on the same level as the doctors. He understood what the defense witnesses were saying—but the jury didn't.

I could tell just from looking at them that they just didn't understand the medical and psychological science.

It was so complicated, in fact, that one juror kept falling asleep during the trial. Head down, nap time.

CHAPTER 6

That bothered me a lot. It looked to me like the jury was bored, like they were tired of the trial after a week and just wanted to go home.

* * *

CHARLOTTE: *You could tell that the jury was lost. They were totally lost. It was just over their heads. They didn't seem to understand what Bob's lawyers were talking about.*

* * *

The defense rested. We were rapidly approaching the finish line.

Brewster, in his closing argument, discussed culpable negligence. He said the jury had to keep in mind that I was a law enforcer, not a trigger-happy guy with a gun.

He compared me to a doctor who makes a mistake during open-heart surgery.

Mistakes are unfortunate, he told the jurors, but they happen.

Now, if a patient dies, do you send the doctor to prison for culpable negligence? If a doctor operates on somebody and nicks an organ or cuts an artery and the patient dies ...

Sure, he's subject to a civil lawsuit. He might even lose his license to practice.

But do you send him to prison?

Of course you don't! If you do, how many people do you think will want to be surgeons? Who would want to be a doctor if they feared being sent to prison for an honest mistake?

It's the same thing with law enforcement, he said. Bob Bates was a certified law enforcement officer, not just some guy with a gun. The "rules" have to be different for police officers. If they're not—if you're going to send them to prison for a mistake—you're not going to have many police officers.

Brewster told the jury that none of the prosecution's witnesses had said I was culpably negligent and that the deputies on the drug task force agreed that Harris's shooting was a mistake. He told the jurors not to condemn me for getting out of my car "to man up and help" my fellow deputies.

"This is somebody we should be proud of, honestly," he said.

As for the cause of death, he repeated what the doctors said: It was "truly coincidental" that Harris had a heart attack right after I shot him.

"The bullet didn't kill him," he said.

* * *

The prosecution got in the last word, and it was short and bitter.

"Do you really need an expert, ladies and gentlemen, to determine what happened to Eric Harris?" Assistant District Attorney John David Luton asked the jury.

"Eight minutes after he's shot, he's dead. Do we need an expert to tell us he died from a gunshot wound?"

* * *

The last man to speak was Judge Musseman. He instructed the jurors that to find me guilty, they had to determine, unanimously and beyond a reasonable doubt, that Harris's death was not an excusable homicide.

According to Oklahoma law,[39] a homicide is excusable:

When committed by accident and misfortune in doing any lawful act, by lawful means, with usual and ordinary caution, and without any unlawful intent.

When committed by accident and misfortune in the heat of passion, upon any sudden and sufficient provocation, or upon a sudden combat provided that no undue advantage is taken, nor any dangerous weapon used, and that the killing is not done in a cruel or unusual manner.

And the jury had to determine whether I was culpably negligent. If I was, they had to find me guilty. If I wasn't, then I was not guilty.

Musseman told the jurors that they had to decide whether what I did was something a prudent individual would have done under the same set of circumstances.

But here's what he didn't tell them, and I think he should have:

My set of circumstances was far from normal. I was a police officer, and police officers hold a special position in our society, one that none of my jurors had ever experienced, and one they could not fully understand.

A police officer, no matter how reasonably prudent, puts his life on the line each and every time he puts on his uniform.

A police officer, no matter how reasonably prudent, puts his life on the line each and every time he puts on his uniform. The dangers a cop faces every day are very different from the ones a prudent schoolteacher or a prudent tax attorney or a prudent software engineer or a prudent trial judge may ever face.

The judge didn't tell that to the jury. I think he should have.

* * *

Six days after the trial started, it now was over.

The jurors left the courtroom to begin their deliberations, and Charlotte, my daughters, Charlotte's sister Terrie, my lawyers, and I went up the stairs to the courtroom where we'd gone during breaks in the trial.

* * *

CHARLOTTE: *The judge was very good to the jurors. He would call for breaks all the time so they wouldn't get too stressed out, and we'd try to find a place where we could get away from the media. We went to the county assessor's office, but they asked us to leave. We finally found refuge in a judge's office. He wasn't there at the time, so this became the place where we'd spend most of our breaks. We'd bring in little sandwiches and try to eat, but it was hard. We were so messed up emotionally.*

* * *

Someone went down to the food stand and brought up some food and snacks. Charlotte and I split a turkey sandwich and a bag of chips, and I had an iced tea, but nothing was going down easy.

Charlotte kept asking me, "Are you OK?" But I wasn't, of course. "I just want this over," I told her over and over again.

Toward the end of the trial, I began to wonder what I would do or what would happen to me if the jury said I was guilty.

Brewster would tell me, "Don't even think about that. That's not going to happen." But how could I not think about it? I was a white deputy who shot a black man. What if I went to prison? Where would I go? Would I be put in general population? Would I be locked up by myself?

Everybody was telling me, "It's going to be all right, it's going to be OK, don't worry about it." But the fact is, I was frightened. There had been so much publicity, and I was sure that if I went to prison, wherever they sent me, some of the inmates there would know my name.

* * *

CHAPTER 6

CHARLOTTE: *I'm a very positive-minded person, and I was still thinking everything's going to be OK.*

I wasn't thinking he'd be going to prison, but I had a pit in my stomach. I was extremely nervous. I just kept thinking about Bob. We were sitting there, and Bob was cutting up a little bit, making a few jokes, but in that room you could feel it was very heavy.

Everybody was trying to make the best of the situation, but not knowing how this was going to come back was very scary. Not knowing whether he'd be going to prison or walking out a free man ... it was an indescribable feeling. I'd never felt anything like it before.

The prosecutors were finished, our attorneys were finished, the judge was finished. Now, all of a sudden, everything was in the hands of twelve people—and they didn't know Bob.

* * *

We sat there for what seemed like forever, and at some point, my lawyers left the room to go talk to the judge. When they came back, it seemed pretty clear that something was wrong.

* * *

CHARLOTTE: *Corbin walked up to Bob and said, "Bob, give me everything in your pockets." Then Bob said, "Charlotte, here, take all my stuff," and he started handing me his billfold, his money, his car keys, everything.*

And I just hugged him and said, "Everything's going to be OK." And he said, "Yeah. I hope so."

I looked at Corbin and asked him, "What's going on?" And he said, "We just need him to have his pockets emptied." But I knew from the look on his face that something was going on, and it wasn't good. You could just tell.

* * *

That's when I thought—for the first time, really—that this thing was about to go south. And a heartbeat later, we got word that the jury had reached a verdict. It had felt like forever sitting there waiting, but we'd been waiting for barely over three hours.

* * *

We walked back down the same staircase we'd gone up, still trying to stay away from the paparazzi. When we got to the fourth floor, there was a crush of people waiting there, lining up to go inside and hear the verdict. I could hardly get through the door.

* * *

CHARLOTTE: *We were just trying to get into the courtroom, and nobody would let us through. We finally got as close as we could to the front when one of the officers came over and told us that we had to get out of the way, that the Harris family was coming through.*

So they let the Harris family go ahead of us, which I thought was odd. Then we finally got through the metal detector. And they wanded us, searched our purses, all of that. Finally, Bob's daughters and I and my sister got through, but it was quite a struggle. There were so many people, and everybody was trying to get in first. It was just awful.

We finally got into the courtroom, and we sat in the first row. Bob was seated at the table in front of us, and it was eerie. It felt like there was just this huge heaviness, a weight in that room. We didn't know what was going to happen, and neither did the Harris family or the press.

They brought the jurors in, and as they walked the ten feet or so to the jury box, they wouldn't look us in the eye. Not even a glance. Suddenly, it got real quiet in the courtroom.

* * *

Judge Musseman came in and asked the jury for its decision. The jury foreman stood up and handed him a little piece of paper. The judge told me to stand up, and he said:

"You're guilty. The jury recommends four years in prison."

* * *

CHARLOTTE: *The judge instructed us that nobody was supposed to make a noise. No clapping, no yelling, nothing—or they'd be put in handcuffs and sent to jail for disrupting the courtroom.*

So the girls and I stayed extremely quiet when they said he was guilty.

But the other side was whooping it up, shouting and yelling. They thought it was great.

I just couldn't understand that. From the minute the shooting happened, everything was horrible for everyone. Eric Harris was dead. Bob was ruined. I just don't understand why anyone would celebrate a man going to prison.

* * *

I just couldn't imagine, after hearing the forensic psychologists and the doctors testify, how the jurors could find me guilty. But they did, and now I was standing there, in the middle of the courtroom, knowing I'd be going to prison. Three deputies immediately came up, put me in handcuffs, and walked me out of the courtroom. They took me to a side door to take the elevator down, then they put me in a sheriff's car and took me about three blocks away to the David L. Moss Correctional Center.

And that was that.

* * *

CHARLOTTE: *My heart just went down into my stomach. I couldn't breathe. I felt like I was going to pass out. I couldn't imagine why they* *found him guilty. I felt that it was a horrible injustice. I just couldn't believe it.*

When they handcuffed him and escorted him out, he passed right by my sister, our daughters, and me, and I just said, "I love you, honey." And he said, "I love you too."

And then he was gone. They got him out of there really quick.

It seemed like my whole life with Bob just flashed before me, and I thought, is somebody going to hurt him in prison? I've been with this man for twenty-four years, every day and every night, and all of a sudden, he's gone. I can't see him, and I'm wondering, will I ever see him again?

After Bob and the jury left, they allowed us to leave. And, of course, we walked outside to chaos. Cameras were everywhere, and everyone was crying, and the Harris family was celebrating, and I just couldn't believe it. I just wanted to say, "You know, you've destroyed this man's life. Why are you happy?"

Bob's daughter Leslie broke down. She was hysterical, and I had to hold her and tell her it was going to be OK. And I believed it, because at that point I thought that he was going to be able to get out on bond.

I told her, "We'll get him out. He's going to get out. Clark will get him out tomorrow."

We were crying, and the media was all over us, and we were just hiding in a corner, until finally I said, "Let's go."

And we went down to the car—Bob's car.

I got inside, but I couldn't drive. I just remember taking my fist and beating on that car as hard as I could. Just beating on it out of frustration.

We drove to Clark Brewster's office. We sat in the conference room—the attorneys, my sister, the girls, and their husbands—and we were in a daze.

And Leslie said, "You've got to do something."

CHAPTER 6

So I asked Clark, "What are we going to do? Do you think you can get him out?"

"No," he said.

"What do you mean?" I asked.

And then he told me that we could not post bond, that Bob could not go home to await his sentencing. In Oklahoma, Clark told me, bond is not permitted if a firearm is the cause of death.

I was stunned, because earlier on, when Bob and I were going to the trial, he told me, "If this thing goes bad, I'll get out in twenty-four hours. Brewster will get me out on bond."

I asked Clark, "What's going to happen now? We want to go see him right now." And he said, "They're going to book him. They're going to put him in jail."

And I said, "Well, when is he going to get out?"

And he said, "Well, he's not getting out. From there, he's going to prison."

* * *

Our daughter Leslie Bates McCrary remembers it this way:

Putting my feelings into words the day they handcuffed my dad has been tough. Every devastating emotion that comes to mind applied that day. It was horrific.

I wanted to scream and yell at the judge and jury that they had it all wrong, it was an accident. At that moment, I think I hated the judge and jury more than I can explain. The judge's behavior throughout the trial was disturbing. So many emotions, none of which I think words could accurately describe.

The second they announced the guilty verdict and put the handcuffs on my dad, I felt like someone had ripped my heart out of my chest and stomped on it with spiked cleats. I remember we were all holding hands,

83

every single one of us in the front two rows of that courtroom, and not letting go until my dad was taken out to be transferred to the county jail.

It felt like an out-of-body experience, where you know it is happening, but it is so horrible you cannot wrap your mind around it. I just kept thinking, surely we are going to wake up from this nightmare, and everything is going to be all right.

* * *

And here's how our daughter Kathy Bates Walter remembers it:
When I heard the judge say the word guilty …

I felt like it wasn't happening. It wasn't real. I don't know if it was just in my head or in the room, but it was completely silent. I didn't hear a sound. I don't believe anyone spoke for the first minute or two, but that could have been my brain shutting down and trying to process.

There was one jury member who showed up on the last day looking very different from the other days of the trial. She had her hair colored, styled, and face made up. It appeared she was prepared for her media debut. All of this started in the media, and it looked like it would finish that way for her as well as others. I do remember shouting to my dad as he walked off, "I love you, Dad, hang in there."

When I returned home, I spent the next couple of days sleeping. I was unable to process the reality, and closing my eyes let me escape momentarily. My brain needed time to catch up. This couldn't be real. I would stop and try to process the reality of what was happening. It was impossible. I would go from tears to problem-solving mode, asking myself, "What is the best-case scenario, and how do we get there?"

As time went on, I learned to cope and handle situations as we faced them. There was always something new, and finding the positive in any aspect was how I chose to face it. I used that mind-set to think clearly, to support my family and my dad the best I could. We didn't have any knowledge or experience in dealing with the justice system, jail, and prison. It seems there are a different set of rules and standards. I learned that quickly when I spoke to someone at the Department of Corrections, before he was transferred from jail to prison. They told me my dad no longer had any rights, and they owned him. This was our new reality.

I had nights where I would wake up in the middle of the night and cry, but after a period of time, I found my new normal and would visit my dad regularly.

* * *

CHARLOTTE: *I don't think there could be anything that could've gotten him free because of what the press did. I strongly believe that. Bob had no voice; he couldn't defend himself.*

We went a full year with nothing but negative press, negative every single day. People talked about a change of venue, but I don't care what venue you had. People were too tainted. We would've had to go to another planet.

I just sat there day after day with Bob's family, his daughters, my sister, our friends and coworkers, people who worked for Bob, and the press, of course. It was very, very difficult to watch him. He was just emotionally drained. And he just wanted it over with.

And when they handcuffed Bob and paraded him right in front of me and the girls, I just remember that I looked at him and told him I loved him. It was very, very difficult, because you don't know what to do. You don't know what's going to happen next. He had suffered so long and so much. It was just awful.

The press killed Bob before the case ever went to trial. They should've just taken him out back and shot him.

7

IT'S AN EASY WALK—only two or three blocks—from the Tulsa County Courthouse to the David L. Moss Correctional Center.

But walking is for people who are free to move about as they please. I was no longer one of them. Walking was not an option.

As soon as the judge declared me guilty of manslaughter, a group of deputies moved in to surround me. They put me in handcuffs and leg irons, whisked me out of the courtroom, and rushed me down the hall to an elevator and then a staircase—that led to the car that took me directly to jail.

> **I was a convicted killer now, a ward of the State of Oklahoma. It would be a long time before I'd be free to walk the streets of my hometown again.**

I was a convicted killer now, a ward of the State of Oklahoma. It would be a long time before I'd be free to walk the streets of my hometown again.

I'd taken a lot of people to the county jail, so I knew my away around. But this time was different: I was the one who'd be left behind.

As soon as I got there, they ran me through a metal detector and took me through a sliding door for booking. They searched me, photographed me, and took my fingerprints. Then they took me to a bathroom down the hall and told me to go inside and put on jail clothing.

I went in wearing a suit; I came out wearing orange pants, an orange shirt, and orange slippers.

My next stop was medical. I walked in, and they looked at me to make sure I was breathing. That was the extent of my entrance physical.

I wondered what they planned to do with a white reserve deputy sheriff who'd been convicted of killing a black man. I was very worried about what might happen to me if they placed me in general population.

But, as it turned out, I had nothing to be afraid of—at least, not yet. They took me upstairs to the medical unit, which has thirty or forty cells, each occupied by a single inmate.

I spent the night there, and in the morning a social worker came by and said she wanted to talk to me.

She asked how I felt about being in jail.

"I'll be honest," I told her. "I'm not very enthused about it."

I said I was concerned about my family and whether they'd be OK while I was behind bars.

The next question she asked was, "Do you feel like hurting yourself?"

I was astonished. "Absolutely not," I said. "I have a wife ... I have two children ... I have six grandchildren. I would have no reason to hurt myself."

Then she left. But pretty soon after that, a couple of guards and a third person—maybe a nurse—came by, grabbed me under the armpits, took me down the hall, stripped me naked, and put me in what they call a "dry cell."

A dry cell has no bed to lie on—not even a mat. There's nothing in there but a toilet and a sink, and they were there for no apparent reason—because they turned off the water.

Later that day, my lawyer arrived to see me. He found me buck naked, talking to him through the hole in the wall where they shoved in my meals. He was appalled.

* * *

They said they were doing all this to protect me—but from what, exactly?

Those orange pants weren't giving me a rash. That orange shirt wasn't cutting off my circulation.

This wasn't about protection. This was all about punishment.

This wasn't about protection. This was all about punishment. I'm certain of that because if they were really trying to protect me—if they were looking out for my well-being—they would have let me have the CPAP machine I use for my sleep apnea. Charlotte and my lawyer brought it to the jail on the day I was booked, but they refused to let me have it for a few nights.

* * *

CHARLOTTE: *Bob didn't know that I was doing this, but I kept calling people to try to get him his CPAP machine.*

Everybody just blew me off until I finally got a hold of the guy who I think was running the show at that time, and I told him, "They have my husband in a cell. He's naked, he has no water, and he doesn't have his breathing machine or any of his medications."

He said, "Oh, I don't know anything about that."

And I said, "Well, you need to go over there and check. He needs to be moved, and if you don't get him the CPAP machine and he quits breathing, it's going to be on you."

He said he'd check it out, and he asked, "What do they have him in a dry cell for?"

I told him, "I have no idea, but he needs his medication. He needs his breathing machine."

That's when they let Bob out of that cell, put him in another one, and finally gave him his breathing machine.

* * *

They gave me some jail pants and a shirt and took me to another cell, where they hooked up the CPAP. There were all kinds of bugs and other things running around in there. I started complaining about it, so after a few days they moved me to a different cell.

And that's where I stayed for almost five weeks—until my sentencing.

* * *

I suppose the medical unit offered me some safety, but the living conditions were horrible. There were only a few men in there who were physically sick. The others were there because of mental issues.

They'd yell and scream and lie on the floor and kick and bang on the doors all night long. And every now and then I'd hear people arguing with the guards, and then *BANG!* I'd hear a Taser go off.

One afternoon, I asked one of the guards, "How often do you shoot that Taser in here?"

"Regularly," she said.

"I've heard it go off a number of times," I said. "Is it really necessary?"

"Oh yes."

CHAPTER 7

She explained that many of the guards were young women—and some of them were pretty small—and there were a few inmates who were perfectly capable of picking them up and slamming them into the floor.

The inmates were behind bars, she said, but the guards had to take them out sometimes, especially if they were misbehaving or trying to injure themselves. And if they resisted, the guards had no choice but to tase them.

At least, that's what she told me. But I think sometimes they tased them just for the hell of it. I think they got their kicks watching those big guys shake and wiggle when they hit the floor.

* * *

Sure, it was called "the medical unit," but I couldn't say why. I had two heart medications—one to keep my blood pressure down, the other to maintain a steady heart rhythm—and I took another pill for anxiety. But I was denied all those medications for several days when I got there.

The unit was in constant lockdown. The inmates weren't allowed out, even for an hour. But one night, after I'd been there for about a week, they woke me up at two in the morning and asked if I wanted to go outside. I said yes, and they took me to the roof. I went out the door and came right back in. It was freezing up there.

The only other time I got out of my cell was when Charlotte came to visit. They would chain me up and take me downstairs to a private visitation area. We were separated by a plexiglass window, and I had to yell to speak with her.

More often than not, they kept me in chains. And after a while, they had to bring me there in a wheelchair, because my knees were badly swollen from the horrible conditions.

* * *

My health was starting to deteriorate. The food was so bad, I ate mostly candy and chips I got from the canteen.

I asked several times to speak with a doctor, but I only got to see one once when I had a stomach issue. They gave me an electrocardiogram and a skin test for tuberculosis, and that was about it. The medical care was just a small step above nonexistent.

But my biggest problems weren't medical. They were boredom and lack of interaction with others. After I'd been there for about a week, I ordered a radio from the canteen. I'd plug it into my ear and lie on my bed and listen all day. That was a real treat.

They also let me do some reading—mostly spiritual books and a Bible.

* * *

CHARLOTTE: *Getting the Bible and spiritual books to Bob was extremely difficult. Pastor Chris Thompson was the only one who could get this done.*

* * *

My cell was an insect's paradise; there were some roaches in there that I'd never seen before, and I started a bug collection. I'd gently step on them and line them up along the wall, because it gave me something to do.

I had to learn how to live with myself, alone, with nobody to touch and nobody to talk to. It wasn't long before I discovered that I was pacing back and forth in my cell.

And I wasn't the only one. Everybody in prison paces back and forth, like animals at the zoo.

For the first time, I understood why lions keep going back and forth in their cages. They're thinking about one thing—getting out.

That's all they want. But they can't. All they can do is pace from one end of the cage to the other. Back and forth, for hours on end.

* * *

Such was my life in jail. I sat in my cell all day, every day, getting out only to see Charlotte or my lawyers, in a room where we were locked in.

My lawyers came to see me, but they didn't have a whole lot to talk about. There was nothing they could do to keep me from going to prison after my sentencing hearing.

The only unknown was whether I would leave prison alive.

* * *

CHARLOTTE: *Bob didn't know this, but I was making call after call because I could see he was in horrible shape. His legs and knees were swollen. They had him chained around his waist and at his ankles, and they made him bend down and stick his arms, with the handcuffs on them, through this hole where they could lock them and unlock them.*

He was beside himself. We had to scream at one another through this plexiglass that had spit all over it, and he kept asking, "Charlotte, what are we going to do?"

He was there for about a week before I got to see him. Two days after he was convicted, I found out that my sister had stage three ovarian cancer and needed a major operation. So I was staying at the hospital with my sister all night, and I would go visit Bob for thirty minutes twice a week.

I would get up and go early in the morning because you had to get on a list, and if you weren't the first one there, you could wait all day. Several times I got there first and wrote my name on the list, and they'd keep knocking me to the back of the list. And I would go up and say, "I was here first, why am I being knocked to the back of the list?"

But I knew the answer: They were harassing me.

You would go in and sign a sheet and give your ID to the people behind the desk. They had lockers there that you paid for. I couldn't take my purse, my cellphone—I couldn't take anything back with me.

I remember it was a very long hallway, and as soon as they said I could go, I just ran as fast as I could down the hallway. Then I went through several doors. Sometimes, I had to wait for them to bring Bob down.

It was just horrible watching him come in there in handcuffs. They would only allow me to see him twice a week—and you could tell he was deteriorating rapidly as the days went on.

I went to our doctor, whom we've been seeing for forty years, and told him how Bob was being treated. He called the jail, and the woman who spoke to him told him snippily, "We're doing the best we can."

And our doctor said, "No, you're not. This man needs to be treated like a human being. He needs his medication."

He was trying to get help for Bob because Bob was being treated worse than the other prisoners. He was in protective custody, which meant he had no rights, no freedom, and no interaction with other people—basically solitary confinement.

He was not allowed out of his cell to do anything because they were afraid somebody would try to kill him. But it's a horrible existence for the man you're trying to protect.

At one point, Bob told me, "Charlotte, I can't stay locked up like this. I can't do it. Tell them I want out. Put me in general custody. I can't do this anymore."

This was abuse, plain and simple. Bob looked worse every time I saw him. He was almost gray in color, and he was dirty because he was allowed to shower only twice a week.

Our lawyer brought Bob some spiritual books, but they told him they might be laced with LSD, so he couldn't bring them in. And this was his attorney!

CHAPTER 7

But there was nothing he could do. Once they slap those handcuffs on, you're just done. Your life does not belong to you anymore. You're not a name, you're a number.

I got in touch with our minister, and he said, "I want to go see him." I asked him, "Can you get him a Bible?" He said he could, and he went through all the paperwork and finally got in to see Bob.

He got in, but the closest he got to Bob was on the other side of that plexiglass window. He brought the Bible, but he couldn't give it to Bob. It was up to the guards to do that.

* * *

I had one other visitor while I was in jail, Deputy Sheriff Ricardo Vaca, the man who secretly recorded the video of me shooting Eric Harris—and the same man who testified against me at my trial.

He showed up unexpectedly to see me one day.

Vaca arrived with someone from the state insurance department who had a letter notifying me that my insurance license had been canceled. After fifty-one years in the business, I couldn't be an insurance agent anymore.

Vaca came into the medical unit and didn't say a word. He just threw the letter under the door to my cell.

I guess he got his jollies that way.

* * *

I was in the county jail for forty-seven days; it seemed like forever. My cell had a small bed—a metal frame with a mattress that was barely two inches thick—a stainless steel sink, and a stainless steel toilet with no seat.

My family, meanwhile, was learning what it was like to have a loved one in the Tulsa County Jail.

* * *

CHARLOTTE: *One day, while I was waiting to be let in to see Bob, a black man came in and said he wanted to fill out the paperwork to go visit someone. The guard behind the desk kept asking him, "Well, who do you want to see? What are you doing?"*

And the guy just said, "All I want is the paper. All I want to do is fill out the paper."

He wasn't yelling; he was talking in a normal tone of voice. But the next thing I knew, two armed guards came out, handcuffed him, and took him to jail—all because he'd asked to fill out an application to go visit one of his relatives.

The guards told him they were arresting him for disturbing the peace.

He kept saying, "I'm not doing anything. All I want to do is fill out the form." And for that, they arrested him. I couldn't believe it.

There was a black woman sitting next to me and I asked her, "Did you see that?"

She said, "Yeah, that's just real typical."

* * *

It may sound hard to believe, but the fact is that as bad as things were for me, I was treated better than so many others in jail—because in Oklahoma, being black just doesn't cut it.

If you're black or Mexican and you're out after ten o'clock at night and there are more than one of you in the car, here's a fact of life: you're going to get stopped. You're going to get harassed. I guarantee it. I saw it firsthand when I was a deputy sheriff.

* * *

On May 31, thirty-four days after I went to jail, I finally got to go outdoors. They took me out of my cell, put me in a Chevy Tahoe,

CHAPTER 7

and drove me back to the Tulsa County Courthouse. The day had arrived for my sentencing hearing.

The last time I was in court, I was wearing a suit. This time, I was in handcuffs and chains, decked out head-to-toe in prison orange. They didn't even let me shower before we left.

The courthouse was packed with reporters who shouted questions at me as they took me down the hall. Their cameras were flashing, and I was in a state of disbelief.

They opened the door to the courtroom, and I walked in. The place was packed. There must have been several hundred people there to see me off to prison.

They marched me up to the bench and sat me down next to my lawyers. My future was now in the hands of one man: Judge William Musseman.

He had it in his power to give me probation, but it was a foregone conclusion that he wouldn't.

The judge came in and everybody stood up.

* * *

CHARLOTTE: *It was very intense. Bob's sister, Julie, flew in from California, and our entire family was there. But we couldn't talk to him. They said they'd arrest us if we did.*

The Harris family was there, too, except for Eric's brother, Andre, and his wife. They were conspicuously absent, and I'm pretty sure I know why.

When Bob was in jail, our attorneys and I thought it would be a good idea for me to meet with the Harris family before the sentencing hearing. I just wanted to talk to them, to tell them how sorry Bob and I were.

I thought we could just talk to each other as human beings, so I had my minister call Andre and his wife, and they said they would meet with me. We arranged to meet at my minister's church or his house, and I was ready to go when my minister phoned and said, "They've canceled. They told me they're going on vacation."

I think they did that because they remembered that Bob had wanted to go on vacation in the Bahamas before his trial. They were saying, "Hey, his life is not important enough for us to show up at this hearing. We're going on vacation." Up until then, Andre Harris was always present.

* * *

The first person the prosecutor called to testify was Cathy Fraley, the mother of Eric Harris's seventeen-year-old son, Aidan.

She had once obtained a protective order against Harris, but now that she was on the stand, she talked about him as if they'd been the happiest couple on earth.

She told the judge what a wonderful father Harris had been, what a great relationship they had, and how when they needed something, he always tended to it.

And my jaw just dropped. Eric Harris had spent most of his adult life in prison. How could they have had a great relationship? How could he have been a great dad?

Well, that's what Cathy Fraley said. And when she got off the stand, I saw her look at the prosecutors, wink, and say, "How'd I do?"

* * *

The next person to testify was Aidan Fraley, Cathy Fraley's son with Harris. He said that losing his father changed his life dramatically and that he was heartbroken that Harris couldn't attend his high school graduation.

"I'll forgive Mr. Bates," he said, "but there are still consequences for your actions."

* * *

Then it was my lawyer's turn. Clark Brewster gave the judge a twelve-page memo arguing that the standard sentence for manslaughter should be probation. But the judge said my case was unique and that the information Brewster had was "misleading."

Brewster brought in a case assessor who interviewed my family, friends, and associates while I was in jail to determine whether I posed a threat to the community.

He told the judge that on a scale of one to forty, I came in at zero. He said putting me in jail would cost the county a lot of money.

Brewster had another man lined up who would testify that three of the jurors in my case had said they were confused when they reached a verdict. But the judge said he had questioned the jurors himself, and he was satisfied that they knew what they were doing. He wouldn't let our witness take the stand.

The most devastating testimony, from my perspective, came from my family physician, Dr. Fred McNeer, a board-certified cardiologist. He told the judge he'd been my doctor for almost forty years and that four years in prison would be like a death sentence.

Dr. McNeer discussed my heart issues and showed pictures of my knees, which were all swollen. He told the judge, "This man will die if you put him in prison. He will die."

* * *

CHARLOTTE: *I called Dr. McNeer. I was trying to get everyone possible to speak for Bob because I thought maybe the judge would be persuaded. There were hundreds and hundreds of letters that were sent to the judge by people in the community who wrote, "Please show mercy on him. He doesn't deserve to go to prison."*

So I called Dr. McNeer and asked him, "Would you please testify?"

He didn't want his name in the paper, but he did it—because he thought what was going on was totally wrong. He told me, "I cannot believe they're treating a human being like this."

* * *

Later in the hearing, Brewster called Charlotte to the stand.

* * *

CHARLOTTE: *He asked me a few questions, and I just remember looking at Bob, and he was in such bad condition, I thought, "Oh my God, he's going to die right here."*

I remember looking at the judge and saying, "Please don't send my husband to prison. I'm not used to begging—I don't beg for anything—but I am standing here now, begging you not to send him to prison. Please."

I begged that man, and he just looked at me and said, "OK, you can get down from the stand now."

Then Clark Brewster really got into it with the judge. He said nobody in the last forty years had been sent to prison for culpable negligence and that sending Bob to jail would set a precedent for every officer in the future.

* * *

Finally, it was my turn to speak. The record shows that I spoke. Charlotte remembers that I spoke, and the newspaper reported I said something.

I don't remember what I said. And whatever it was, nobody could hear it.

* * *

CHARLOTTE: *He could barely whisper. He didn't have a mic on, and we were in a big courtroom. No one could hear him say he was sorry and ask for mercy.*

CHAPTER 7

* * *

The hearing lasted four hours. Near the end, my lawyer and the judge went to the back of the room and had a little conference.

Then the judge came back and sentenced me to serve four years in prison—the maximum sentence.

* * *

CHARLOTTE: *He was very matter of fact, like it was no big deal. And on the other side of the courtroom, Eric Harris's family and his supporters were cheering and high-fiving.*

They took Bob out, and I went over and hugged Eric's son. I told him, "I'm so sorry about your dad."

And he hugged me back, and he said, "I'm really sorry."

I said, "I know you are."

And then I looked at the prosecutor and I said, "This is nothing to be happy about. You've just ruined a man's life and probably killed him."

The prosecutor looked at me and said, "I can say whatever the hell I want to say."

One of the attorneys in Brewster's law firm saw what was going on, and she came over and grabbed me. She said, "Charlotte, they're going to put you in jail."

And she dragged me out of there. I went out in the hall, and everyone was just going crazy. People were crying. People were cheering. Bob's daughter Leslie just broke down.

* * *

I didn't see any of that. I was already in a Tahoe, heading back to jail for a short stay before they took me to prison.

8

YOU DON'T GO DIRECTLY to prison in the state of Oklahoma. Sure, you're on a one-way road to a small cell—whether you think you belong there or not—but you'll have to make some mandatory pit stops before you get there.

The first place they took me after my sentencing was to the one I was so happy to leave earlier that day: my tiny cell in the Tulsa County Jail. Once again, I had no idea how long I'd have to remain there, but I was certain about where I'd be going next: Lexington, a small city that's just two and a half square miles, population 2,100, in the geographical center of Oklahoma. It's about a two-and-a-half hour drive from Tulsa, and, even though I'd lived in Oklahoma for more than seven decades, I'd never been there.

Now, I was going, like it or not, because Lexington is where the state built the Lexington Assessment and Reception Center, a "preprison prison" that has been receiving and assessing convicted male felons in Oklahoma since 1978.

You can't go to prison without first going to Lexington, and you can't go to Lexington until someone decides to take you there. And exactly when that would happen was anyone's guess.

But once you're there, you may spend four, six, even eight weeks before the state decides where to send you next.

I lingered in the psych ward at the county jail for nine more days until the early morning of June 9, when, as soon as I finished my breakfast, two sheriff's deputies showed up at my cell door, chained me up, and put me in a car.

They cuffed me tight enough to cut off the circulation to my hands and leave cuts and bruises on my wrists. They were taking no chances—they brought a shotgun along, just in case.

And just like that, after forty-seven days in jail, I was on my way to Lexington Assessment Center.

* * *

CHARLOTTE: *I wanted Bob to know what to expect. I didn't want him to be thrown in there without knowing what was going on. So I started making calls, dozens of them. The people at Lexington Assessment Center told me Bob would be put in isolation for no less than six weeks and that he would not be allowed anything except a toothbrush and a bar of soap, which they would provide.*

I couldn't bring him something to read, and I would not be allowed to see him.

They told me they knew Bob was coming, but they didn't know what they were going to do with him. They said they were shocked that he was going there. They couldn't believe he'd been sentenced to prison. They couldn't believe he was guilty.

They told me Lexington is where they take prisoners to see if they're nuts, if they've murdered someone, how violent they are. They already knew who Bob was. Going to Lexington was just another form of punishment.

I went to the jail to tell Bob what was going to happen, and he started crying. He said, "What am I going to do? I can't be locked down anymore. I can't do this anymore."

I said, "I'm telling you what's going to come down so you can be ready for it." It was so horrible seeing Bob go through all this. When I left I cried as well.

* * *

The first thing they did when I got to the assessment center was shave my head and conduct a total body search. Then they gave me a dental exam and what they referred to as "a physical." I reached out to shake hands with the doctor, but he refused. He said he didn't shake hands with prisoners.

Then they took me upstairs to a maximum-security unit and put me in a cell that had nothing but the absolute necessities. Despite the insufferable heat of an Oklahoma summer, there was no air conditioning. It was not an absolute necessity. It felt like an oven.

Our pastor at home in Tulsa told Charlotte he would ask the pastor at the assessment center to bring me a Bible and to pray with me.

The pastor never did bring me a Bible, but he did come to my cell. He prayed with me, and I told him how hot it was and that I was honestly worried about heatstroke.

He just looked at me and said, "Well, that's too bad. You're going to have to stay here at least four to six weeks, so you better get used to it."

I'd been sentenced to four years in prison—not twenty-three hours a day for four to six weeks in an unforgivably hot cell—but the heat wasn't my greatest discomfort.

Word had spread very quickly that I was there. Everybody knew who I was—and I was worried that some of the men there would try to kill me.

The prisoners at the assessment center were free to walk around the cellblock, and they took advantage of their "freedom" to walk up to my locked cell and slide threatening notes under the door.

On my very first day, four of them tried to kick my door down. When they discovered they couldn't burst through, they started kicking the door's plexiglass window, which was big enough for any of them to get through.

They were running at it and kicking it, and even though they were wearing tennis shoes, I wasn't sure it would hold.

Out of fear, I shouted, "I'll cut you if you come through that window." They finally gave up trying.

Compared to that, the heat was a picnic.

* * *

Something good actually came out of that incident. The notes those four guys slid under my door made their way to someone of authority, and she and a guard came to my cell the next morning, opened my door, and transferred me to an area where I'd be safe—the wing where they put sex criminals.

I was confined to my cell, but I spoke to some of the prisoners in that wing through my door, and they were very decent. They weren't violent; they were just waiting to be sent to a prison.

There were a couple of guys there who I thought were girls, and I could hear them singing at night. They were really good. Every now and then I'd call out for an encore.

I stayed there for four days. I got out once to take a shower and another time to call Charlotte on the phone downstairs. Other than that, I just sat in my cell. It was every bit as hot as the first cell they put me in, but at least I felt safe.

* * *

CHAPTER 8

The four to six weeks the pastor said I'd be at the assessment center ended up lasting only five days. After one night in general population and four in the sex criminal section, I was finally going to where a judge and jury said I belonged—the Joseph Harp Correctional Center, a medium-security prison.

The trip lasted all of four minutes—three-tenths of a mile east on Route 39, eight-tenths of a mile north on 156th Street, and just over half a mile east on Moffat Road. Joseph Harp is in Lexington.

The warden and the chief of security met me at the front door, and they took me to the mental health unit, a fenced-in part of the prison that consisted of two buildings, side by side. They thought I'd be safer there.

And this time—for the first time since I was found guilty and whisked off to jail—I would be sharing a cell.

My roommate was Jerome Ersland, a pharmacist in his midsixties who shot a teenage gang member to death in 2009 when the gang tried to rob his Oklahoma City store at gunpoint.

The men were black. Ersland was white. He pleaded not guilty, arguing that he had fired in self-defense, but a jury convicted him of murder in 2011 with life sentence. He'd been in Joseph Harp for five years.

Like me, Ersland was an aging white man who'd been convicted of killing a black man, and he needed to be separated from the general population because at least one of his victims had been a gang member. His fellow inmates were threatening retribution.

He and I had a lot in common. They didn't know what to do with either of us, so they put us together in an eight-by-ten cell.

* * *

We were allowed out of our cells every now and then. They'd lock us in a cage that was about eight feet wide and twelve feet long with a roof over it, and we'd walk back and forth in there like lions at the zoo for about forty-five minutes. Then they'd come back, unlock the doors, and put us back in our cell.

We were allowed to do this only when everyone else was locked down and only when we weren't in the middle of a count, which is something that happens whenever there's a potential problem. It's what they do to make sure nobody's gone over a wall, jumped over a fence, been stabbed, or whatever.

A count can take an hour or it can take all day. A few months later, when I was transferred to the North Fork Correctional Center in Sayre, someone got killed in an adjoining building the first night I got there, and seven more guys were beat up and stabbed. They locked us down for a full twenty-four hours.

Ersland was very helpful to me. Whether I was in our cell or in the cage, I did a lot of pacing, and he told me he did the same thing when he got there. He had some bad experiences too. One time he was in the yard, and guys started throwing rocks at him. That scared the hell out of him, and he asked to be put into protective custody.

So he and I were in this together, and that was good for both of us because prison really affects you mentally. You're in a constant battle with depression. Before I got there, I had hoped that I wouldn't be locked in my cell all day and that I'd be able to go out and do social things, like playing cards, checkers, and various board games.

I'd be in general population, but I was willing to take that risk. I figured I could get along, and I told the warden I was more than happy to try it.

Evidently, they weren't—but at least they gave me a roommate I could talk to. And after nearly two months of what amounted to solitary confinement, that was a real relief.

It was for Ersland as well. Like me, he was well educated, and he didn't have anyone to talk to until I showed up.

* * *

CHARLOTTE: *I finally got to visit Bob on June 16 after I made a million phone calls and found the people who could get me in. I drove the two-and-a-half hours from Tulsa for my 2 p.m. visit, and then they made me wait two hours before they finally let me in. Bob's daughters were with me, but they weren't going to let them in because they didn't have special permission. I explained that one of them had come all the way from Texas. Finally, the assistant warden let us all go in.*

They took our purses, made us take our shoes off, and wanded us like they do at the airport. Then they patted us down and made us wait one more time before they let us go through two more locked doors.

We were in a room that looked like a cafeteria, but nobody was in there except Bob. He was crying. He looked very sad and very scared, and he told me about the gang that tried to break into his cell at the assessment center. He said he was still afraid that someone would try to kill him.

He was wearing a taupe-gray uniform, and he looked like he'd lost about twenty pounds. His head was shaved, and he had red bites all over his chest. He said he was very concerned about bedbugs.

The warden came in, and he seemed to really care about the prison and the prisoners. I told him about the gang that tried to kill Bob at the assessment center, and he seemed very surprised. He said he'd call the warden who moved Bob to another cell.

But ultimately, they all denied that any of it happened. It was Bob's word against the warden's. And Bob was a convicted killer.

We were trying to get Bob some basic things he needed because we were very concerned about his mental and physical health. He was spiraling downhill. He was losing weight. He couldn't eat. He was sick to his stomach. He had these bites all over him.

He also had a horrible rash because there was no toilet seat in his cell. Every time he sat down, his butt went into the water.

I had to work with the warden just to get him a toilet seat.

* * *

I'd been at Joseph Harp for just two or three days when three black men came to my door.

It had been only about a week since the incident at the assessment center, and my first thought was, "Uh-oh, here we go again. I'm in trouble."

But this time it was different. I sat on the floor and talked to them through the bean hole in the door, and they said they had come to welcome me to the penitentiary. They said if there was anything they could do for me, they'd be more than happy to do it. They came around on a fairly regular basis, and we became friends.

Two of the guys were from Tulsa, and one was an ordained minister. One day, I asked him if there was a chance I could be baptized.

About two months later—with a guard watching every step because they were afraid someone would try to beat my ass—I was taken with two other prisoners to a room where there was a little church arrangement, and the three of us were submersed in a tub and baptized.

CHAPTER 8

If there was one good thing that came out of my time in prison, it was this. Being baptized gave me a relationship with God and Jesus. I felt really good about it, and I still do. I think that without God watching over me in prison, I might not have made it.

* * *

It was interesting being in the cell. At night, there were little field mice that would get into bed with you. Three or four times a week, I'd feel them running up my leg and would throw them against the wall to get them to leave.

There were some inmates who didn't mind the mice at all. Some even adopted them as pets. They'd break up some crackers and kneel on the floor, waiting for one to come out. When it did, they'd throw a T-shirt over the mouse—and then they had it.

They'd train them by putting them in the toilet and letting them swim around until they almost drowned, and then they'd save them. Strangely enough, after two or three weeks of this, the mice didn't want to leave the inmate who'd been torturing them.

The guys would walk around with a mouse in their pocket, and every now and then it would peek out.

Of course, if you wanted a pet mouse and didn't want to go through the process of training it, you always had the option of buying one. A trained mouse sold by other inmates went for five bucks. I didn't want one, but I had plenty of access to one if I did.

There was one prisoner who found another use for the mice.

One day, after I was allowed to go outside, I was out in the grass area and saw a guy pick up a mouse, bite its head off, and chew it up.

"Not bad," he said.

Then he ate the back part, spat it out and said, "Tastes like shit."

It's hard to believe, but that kind of stuff is normal in prison. I remember one guy who would walk outside every evening and stand on the sidewalk, then the grass, then the sidewalk, then the grass. And the whole time he was doing this, he'd say out loud, "I'm on the concrete, I'm on the grass, I'm on the concrete, I'm on the grass."

That was his evening routine.

Another time, I was outside in the afternoon and a couple of guys got into a fight. One of them was already bleeding when the other guy went inside, got a pen with a plastic tip that he'd sharpened as a weapon, came back out, and stabbed him in the neck, trying to hit his carotid artery. There was only one guard there, and when he finally got things under control, they took the guy who got stabbed to the medical facility and patched him up.

There was another prisoner there who found a unique way to attempt suicide: he shoved a light bulb up his butt and then crushed it. The guards came running down to get him, and he put up such a fight that they had to use pepper spray to subdue him.

I wish I could say that these things were unusual, but things like these happened all the time.

* * *

The guards had big canisters of pepper spray for ending fights and subduing out-of-control prisoners, and the stuff was very effective—sometimes too effective. I knew a few things about pepper spray, and if they'd asked me, I would have given them my two-step guide for how to use it:

Never use pepper spray indoors.

See number one.

CHAPTER 8

One day while I was at Joseph Harp, a guard used pepper spray to end a disturbance in a cellblock, and, sure enough, it got into the recirculating air system and found its way into my cell.

It nearly killed Ersland. He pretty much stopped breathing, and I screamed out for help and started beating on his chest, trying to get him going. I was about to perform mouth-to-mouth resuscitation when one of the guards opened our door. I dragged Ersland out, pulled him up the stairs, and took him outside. He retched and gagged and finally came around. And then the prison officials said it never happened. They claimed they didn't use pepper spray. They said it was all a lie. I even gave them the names of the guards who were involved, but they denied everything.

Ersland had been keeping records since the day he got there, and he told me this was the eleventh time he'd seen this happen. He knew the incidents, but the guards and the warden said they never happened.

This was significant to me because there's a rule or policy that if you save an inmate's or a guard's life, or you do something remarkably helpful and wonderful within the prison, they award you points that come off of your sentence. I felt I deserved points for saving Ersland's life—but how can you for something they say never happened?

* * *

About two months into my time at Joseph Harp, one of the supervisors came to me and said they could use some help with a few things. I very quickly said yes. I knew that if I had work to do, I'd get to leave my cell.

They had these garments they called "suicide suits," which were kind of like straitjackets. Every time someone tried to kill himself—something that happened regularly—they'd put him in a suicide suit for a while. When they finally took it off, it would have to be cleaned and ready for the next guy. They wanted me to help the guy in charge of washing them.

I was also asked to help empty the trash, which meant I'd get to walk outside the guardhouse. The first time, I asked the guards to open the gate, and they wouldn't do it. They called on the radio and said, "There's an inmate out and he's carrying some stuff with him." The reply they got was, "That's Bates, he's just taking out the trash."

From there on out, they opened the gate for me every morning so I could take out the garbage, and I reached a point where they trusted me, and I could go wandering around within our compound. Finally, I could get some exercise, which was good for both my body and mind. It made me feel better. But it didn't last long.

* * *

When Charlotte found out I wouldn't be getting any points for saving Ersland's life because the warden and guards were saying they never used pepper spray, she arranged to meet with Joe Allbaugh, who had served as FEMA director for President George W. Bush and was now the director of the Oklahoma Department of Corrections.

She went with my daughter Leslie, and it did not go well.

* * *

CHARLOTTE: *We went to him because Bob wasn't being treated like the other prisoners. He wasn't getting the freedoms they were getting, and he'd saved Ersland's life and wasn't getting any credit for it.*

So we went to Allbaugh.

I gave him the names of the guards who saw Bob save Ersland's life. He said it never happened.

All of a sudden, he accused us of asking for favors. We said we weren't looking for any favors; we just wanted Bob to be treated like everyone

CHAPTER 8

else. I told him Bob was a very social man, a smart man with a degree who had asked prison officials if he could teach GED classes, but they wouldn't let him.

He can help, I said, but you're locking him away in a cage, and it's hurting everyone—not only Bob but the inmates who need better education.

He was so rude. He said he was going to check into my complaints—and the next thing I knew, my husband disappeared. He was just gone. I called the prison, and they told me they didn't know where he was.

Do you know how that feels? For all I knew, they'd carried him away in a body bag.

* * *

Charlotte left angry, and Leslie left crying. Every time a newspaper asked Allbaugh about me, he said I was able to go to the recreation area and that I was free to do whatever I wanted with the other inmates.

That was just a flat-out lie. What was worse was that Allbaugh was keeping tabs on me. Prison employees told me he was asking about me and Ersland—and soon after Charlotte and Leslie met with him, we were put in separate cells.*

A few days later, two captains came around in the morning and said, "Come on, let's go." They handcuffed me, chained me up, and took me down to a cell that was about two feet by two feet, just enough room for a chair.

---

* The following story was published in the June 13, 2019 edition of The Tulsa World by Barbara Hoberock:" Department of Corrections Director Joe M. Allbaugh abruptly resigned Wednesday during a Board of Corrections meeting. His resignation came after the newly constituted board elected officers. Allbaugh took personal privilege to address the board. His resignation was not on the agenda. Allbaugh said. "For the last three years, five months and four days, I have had the honor of leading this organization, rightly or wrongly." Allbaugh is gone, thankfully. I believe he wasn't qualified to run Oklahoma's prison system.

115

They left me there for a couple of hours. Soon, a couple of transportation guards showed up in a van to take me away. We were heading west. They sat up front. They wouldn't talk to me.

They stopped for lunch, and I told them I needed to use the bathroom.

"You can't," they said.

"I've had prostate surgery," I said, "and I have to go frequently. What am I supposed to do?"

"That's your problem."

When they came back, one of them was drinking from a plastic bottle. I told him if he didn't give me that bottle when he was done with it, I was going to piss in the van. So he gave it to me. It's almost impossible to get your pants down while you're sitting in a van with chains around your waist, but I eventually succeeded. By the time we got to our destination, I badly needed to go again.

* * *

By then, it was the afternoon, and I was far to the west—in Sayre, three and a half hours from Tulsa. It's just twenty miles east of Texas at the North Fork Correctional Center, a medium-security prison that houses 2,500 inmates.

I got out of the van in the garage next to general population, where there were around two hundred prisoners. They were about to turn me loose when I piped up and said, "I don't think I belong in there. I'm supposed to be in protective custody."

This apparently was news to them, but they called in to check, and when they got off the phone, they took me away and locked me up in a cell where I'd be safe. And soon enough, after they put me there, who do I see walking past my cell?

It was Ersland.

CHAPTER 8

I said, "What the hell? How did you get here?"

And he said, "I just got here."

Neither of us were told we'd be transferred to North Fork, and neither of us knew that the other guy was going. It was pure punishment, and it was obvious. After Charlotte and Leslie visited Allbaugh, they decided to separate Ersland and me and move us to North Fork in two vans because it was farther from our homes. For Charlotte, it would mean driving seven hours roundtrip from Tulsa to see me.

Even worse was that they never bothered to tell Charlotte that I'd been transferred, and they put me back in a twenty-four-hour lockup for several days, letting me out only once to take a shower.

* * *

CHARLOTTE: *They just moved him. I didn't know where he was, and I was freaking out. No one would tell me anything.*

Finally, I got a call from Bob. He was obviously scared, and he told me, "My God, they've got me locked down again in this tiny cell. I can't do this, Charlotte."

I said, "OK, let me see what I can do." I made some calls and got connected to Greg Kinnison, who was in charge of a group of cellblocks that had more than three hundred inmates.

I can't say enough good about him. I asked him if I could talk to Bob, and he said, "Yeah, let me go to his cell." He was kind enough to hand Bob the phone through the cell door and let me talk to him for a few minutes.

Then he found a cell where Bob wouldn't be in a twenty-four-hour lockup. He asked me, "Do you think he'd mind being in a handicapped cell?" I told him Bob wouldn't mind at all.

* * *

Sayre was an interesting place. Whenever Charlotte and my daughters came to see me, they would clear the yard and march me out across the prison grounds to the visitor center. My family had to walk a long way too—in the cold, sometimes in the rain—to get there. And they weren't allowed to wear their coats. They had to leave them behind.

* * *

CHARLOTTE: *The visitor's room was just nasty. They brought Bob in, and he looked awful. His skin was gray, his hair was dirty, his nails were very long—and now he was in North Fork with a lot of gang members, and all we could think was that he really wasn't going to come out of there alive.*

* * *

The first night I was there, a man who I gathered was representing the black inmates showed up and said he wanted to know what I was all about.

I told him, "I'm not a racist. I don't have any problems with anybody: black, yellow, purple, green, doesn't make any difference."

And that was the truth, no matter what some folks in Tulsa might have thought. I know who I am, and I know what's in my heart, and that was the plain and simple truth.

We talked for a long time, and the next morning, he brought me a grapefruit—which meant a lot because fresh fruit is hard to find there. And sure enough, we became friends.

I was in the general population now, and I was happy to be there. We were in lockdown a lot of the time, but at least we were allowed to leave our cells when we weren't. And from time to time, depending on the weather and the attitude of the guards, we were allowed to go out to the recreation area. I can't even describe how disgusting it was.

CHAPTER 8

There was bird crap everywhere, on the basketball courts, even on the outside toilets.

But at least it was outdoors. I could look up and see the sky.

And despite the circumstances that had landed me in prison, I was making friends. As I was having trouble walking, someone always took a chair outside for me so I wouldn't have to sit on the ground. It was almost always a young Mexican guy. He'd take the chair out for me so that I didn't have to carry it.

They even started to give me nicknames: "OG," for Original Gangster, Old Guy, Old Man. They also called me "Dr. Phil" because I found myself counseling a lot of them when they were suffering from depression.

* * *

Now don't get me wrong, North Fork was no country club. One morning, I opened my cell door, and the black and Mexican populations were having some problems. Many of them met in the middle of the cellblock, and the fight was on. About twenty-five guys were involved, and it got pretty violent.

The guards did what they always do in those circumstances: they got the hell out of there because the guys had knives. The inmates would somehow get their hands on a clipboard, rip off the metal clip at the top, sharpen the clip with sandpaper until it was a well-honed knife, and they'd fashion a handle with whatever tape they could find.

And just as the two sides were getting into it, my inmate friend came at me, pushed me back into my cell, and slammed the door. He said, "I don't want you involved in this."

Pretty soon after that, one of the guards came back with pepper spray and began spraying it everywhere. Several of the guys, including me, were having trouble breathing, so they opened the door after they gained control of the situation and let us out.

One of the guys had heart trouble and was throwing up, so I went to the medical station and told the person who was there—a nurse of some kind—that I needed a canister of oxygen for the guy.

"We don't have any," the nurse said.

"No oxygen in a place like this?"

"Nope."

I went back out, and the guy was on his knees, still throwing up, and I just stood there patting him on the back. There was another guy with asthma who was having trouble breathing, and I was too. At least the guards were nice enough to bring us a couple of chairs.

> **I was by far the wealthiest person there, and I was well educated—so I put my money and my college degree to good use helping my fellow inmates.**

It was pretty rough in there the rest of the afternoon, but I guess you could say it's the kind of thing that happens pretty often in prison. I'd witnessed it two or three times at Joe Harp, and now I was seeing it at North Fork.

But here's what was really disturbing: while I was sitting there coughing up a lung, I heard two new guards say they could hardly wait to use their pepper spray.

I told them, "Guys, that's not good. It's gonna blow back on you, and you're gonna be gagging and retching right along with the guys you're spraying." But they were having none of that. They just wanted to use that pepper spray.

CHAPTER 8

The dumbest thing I saw there was a deputy who was in a car with a prisoner who started acting up, and he sprayed him in the car. That was not a smart move.

* * *

I realized that what happened to me that day—the guy pushing me back into my cell to keep me safe—was a sign of respect and appreciation from my fellow inmates that I worked hard to earn during my time at North Fork.

I was by far the wealthiest person there, and I was well educated—so I put my money and my college degree to good use helping my fellow inmates.

A lot of them couldn't read or write, so I helped them craft letters for various court filings to apply for parole or have their sentences reduced.

I offered to teach reading, writing, and GED classes, because illiteracy is a big problem in prison. But they wouldn't let me because you got credit for everything that was education related. If you took a class, you got credit. If you taught a class, you got credit. When I was at Joseph Hart, I actually got the OK to attend a couple of classes—but then they jerked me out of there and sent me to North Fork.

I also did some counseling for inmates. A lot of guys get it in their heads that their lives are worthless, and they become deeply depressed.

There was a young man at Harp whom I saw coming down the stairs one day, and he was crying. I said, "OK, what's wrong?" He told me he wanted to give me all his property.

Uh-oh. Property is a big thing in prison. You don't give it away if you're planning to stick around. "I know what you're thinking," I told him, "and we're not going there."

We went over to my cell, sat down, and talked. "You're a young man," I said. "You're due to get out of here in a couple or three years. You have family. You're not thinking sensibly."

We sat and talked for a while about home, girlfriends, and whatnot, and then he seemed to calm down and started feeling better about things. We talked about a girl he really liked, about his grandmother. I said, "What do you think she's going to think if you're not here?" After a while I told him, "I want you to go on back to your cell and think about this. I'll check on you here in a little bit."

It took a while, but he turned it around. I visited with him almost every day when we were allowed out.

I also put my money to good use for others. I made coffee and I kept a lot of Advil and Pepto-Bismol, which so many of them needed because the food was just horrible, and they kept getting diarrhea and stomach ailments.

These products are some of the many things that any inmate can buy at the canteen, and everyone is allowed to spend up to one hundred dollars a week there. But you can't buy anything if you don't have money.

I was lucky. I had money.

* * *

I had a good attitude too. Maybe I was just stupid, but when I got to North Fork and they took me out of lockdown and let me mix with the other prisoners, I was unbelievably happy because socialization is so important. And I thought if I could do one good thing every day that might change somebody's life even just a little bit, I'd feel good going to bed at night.

Sure, I had trouble with a few of the prisoners. I'd tell them, "Don't consider me to be weak and think you're going to take advantage of me, because I will hit you in the head just as hard as I can. I may come out on the bottom, but I'll tell you what—you won't walk out of here without blood all over you. I can promise you that."

I think they respected that. I was over seventy years old, and I was willing to get into a fight with a guy of twenty-two. I was ready to stand up for myself, *so don't mess with me.*

And besides, they really did like my coffee.

9

I WALKED OUT of prison on October 19, 2017—two and a half years after I shot Eric Harris, a year and a half after I was found guilty of manslaughter. I spent 540 days behind bars—47 in the Tulsa County Jail and 497 at Joe Harp and North Fork.

A lot of people, including me, thought I never should have been arrested, let alone found guilty. But a lot of others wanted nothing more than to see me rot in prison for the rest of my life—until I was taken out in a coffin.

My detractors were denied that satisfaction, but let's make one thing clear:

I got no special treatment. Nobody did me any favors.

I was charged and found guilty of manslaughter, I was given the maximum sentence of four years in prison, and I was released after serving "only" 37 percent of that sentence because that's how things work in Oklahoma.

I was a first-time offender, I was a model inmate, and the Oklahoma Department of Corrections gives prisoners "credits" for good behavior and participation in certain programs that reduce their prison time.

But I learned a lot during my eighteen months in prison, and I came out a very different man from the one who went in.

Though I had arrested or participated in the arrests of scores of men during my years as a deputy sheriff, I never really understood how the criminal justice system works—and how it fails consistently—until I was the one in handcuffs.

* * *

I went into the criminal justice system blind, and I came out with my eyes open wider than I ever might have imagined. I'm in the unique position of having seen it from both sides of the prison gate, and this is what I've concluded:

> **Everyone who has a hand in sending someone to prison should be required to spend a few weeks behind bars himself.**

Everyone who has a hand in sending someone to prison should be required to spend a few weeks behind bars himself.

And I really do mean everyone—every sheriff, every deputy, every cop, every judge, every lawyer, every prison guard, every governor, senator, congressman, mayor, and local politician.

I don't mean a social visit. I mean real incarceration, "undercover," their real identities unknown to everyone inside, from the warden on down—because only then will they understand that everything about our prisons is broken and that the people in charge are unwilling or unable to fix things because they don't really understand what they're in charge of.

They need to become actual prisoners so they can see it, hear it, and feel it for themselves.

CHAPTER 9

Local and state officials occasionally make headline-grabbing visits to prisons to get to the bottom of something or other—but whatever they find, it's lightyears from reality.

One day, when I was at Joe Harp, a state legislator paid us a "fact-finding" visit. But what he saw was a joke.

Nobody told him that a group of inmates stayed up the entire night before he showed up, getting everything clean and polished and putting some other things away where he wouldn't see them.

The next day, he came through the gate and walked around a bit—but only a bit. As soon as he started heading toward my building, the deputy warden announced, "Come on, we've got to get lunch."

My building was the mental ward, and the deputy warden not only wanted to keep the legislator out—she didn't want him getting anywhere near it, because the guys in there are liable to do anything. They'll stand around buck naked, they'll throw stuff at you … Nobody wants a legislator to see any of that.

In fact, nobody even wanted the guy to eat the same food the prisoners ate. They took him to the employee cafeteria.

I don't know what that legislator told everyone he learned in his "fact-finding" mission, but I'm certain about one thing: it wasn't the facts.

* * *

If you want to know the facts, you need to do more than visit. You need to stay a while.

If you're the governor, you may get to know the terror of sharing an eight-by-ten cell with a lunatic who just might be in the mood to stab you in the neck.

If you're a senator, you may find out what it's like to spend twenty-three hours a day alone in your cell for a couple of weeks, with only mice and insects to keep you company.

If you're the sheriff or the mayor or a congressman or a state legislator, you may find out what it's like to spend a couple of weeks in a filthy environment, surrounded by senseless violence and drugs, unable to touch or even see a loved one.

You'll find out what it's like to have a choice between starving and eating inedible food.

Get a toothache, come down with an intestinal illness, develop a fever, and you'll learn all about inadequate medical care.

Stay a couple of weeks and you won't have to imagine any of this. You'll figure out what you should have known all along—that no man can improve himself in this environment.

And if you're one of those folks who like to puff out their chests and say, "If you can't do the time, don't do the crime" … if you think criminals are no better than animals and so they deserve to be treated like animals …

Well, if that's what you think, then you should think about this too:

Very few prisoners are doing life without parole. At some point, most of them will be released.

And when they're released, I promise you:

Almost every one of them will come out more dangerous than when he went in. He'll be more violent, more drug-addicted, more willing to inflict pain on others—and his victims could very well be you and your loved ones.

* * *

CHAPTER 9

There's so much that needs fixing, it's almost hard to know where to begin. But if there's one issue that stands above all others, it's the pervasive and soul-crushing violence that permeates every moment of incarceration.

My first night in North Fork, a gang fight broke out a couple of cellhouses down from where they took me, and seven guys were stabbed. They brought in helicopters in the morning to take a guy or two out, and the rest went in ambulances.

Except for one guy. He didn't make it.

North Fork had three cellhouses with big glass windows at one end so you could look out and see what was going on in the other two. One day I saw a guy step out of the shower and start heading back to his cell when a guy with a knife came up and cut him in the neck. He was going for the carotid artery.

Another time, I was looking out the window when I saw a guard taking a prisoner out of his cell, and all of a sudden, the guy hauled off and hit him. The guard went down, and the prisoner grabbed his pepper spray and sprayed him good.

A group of guys were watching with me, and they were fascinated. They were clapping their hands … whooping it up …

In prison this qualifies as entertainment.

* * *

At Joe Harp, I was put in the mental ward for my protection, and I found out pretty quickly that nobody knows what those guys in there are going to do. I'm not sure even *they* know what they're going to do.

One day, I was standing outside with some guys when, out of the blue, someone just hauled off on a guy about two people away from me. He practically knocked him out.

Why? Just because.

I remember another guy—a young guy—at Joe Harp who was very afraid of some inmates who were threatening him, so he asked the deputy warden to move him to a different cellblock.

She said no.

A few days later, four guys got into the kid's cell and stomped him bad.

When they finally stopped, his head was the size of a large watermelon, and I thought, "He's going to be dead, I guarantee it, in the next forty-eight to seventy-two hours."

And I was right. They just beat him to death.

Another time, a couple of guys got into a big fight. I didn't see it start, but I saw how it ended. I was standing outside when they came around the corner, and one of the two, a big man who had very little to say, went back to his cell to get his shank—a makeshift knife he fashioned by taking the ink cartridge out of a ballpoint pen and sharpening the barrel.

He'd already beaten the smaller guy up—he left the kid standing in the yard, needing medical attention—when he came back and stabbed him in the neck.

The guard—the only one there, assigned to cover two cellhouses—picked up a baton and went out to try to shut things down, and the guys just stood there, looking at each other. Finally, the big guy put down his shank.

They transferred him to the cell next to mine, so I had the chance to talk to him now and then. He'd ask for the time, so I'd tell him.

He was a real mess—a danger to everyone—and wouldn't you think a "correctional" system would try to help him get corrected?

That would be very wishful thinking.

And that's the thing that's impossible to believe—until you've been in prison and actually seen it for yourself:

CHAPTER 9

This is normal. This stuff happens. Somebody gets mad … somebody has a few screws loose … and the next thing you know, somebody's getting beaten to a pulp or stabbed—or killed.

* * *

A lot of the prisoners have shanks. They'll make a knife out of anything they can get their hands on.

A friend of mine told me he was stabbed seventeen times in a previous incarceration. They figured he'd die, but he lived to talk about it—and his attitude about what happened was just astonishing:

He said getting stabbed was just one of the hazards of being in prison. Nothing unusual about it. It's just violence.

* * *

Sometimes, a small guy gets it in his head that he can beat the crap out of a big guy, and then he gets a bit too aggressive and winds up paying the price.

That's another thing to remember in prison: the bigger guy usually comes out on top.

One of my friends told me that he once had a cellmate he didn't like, so he told the guard, "Get him out of here, he's driving me crazy."

The guard told him, "Show me some blood," and walked away.

So that's what my friend did. He knocked the guy down to the floor, kicked him in the head with his boots, yelled for the guard to come back, and told him, "Here's your blood."

That stuff is plain crazy—but for a lot of inmates, it's the entertainment portion of the day.

* * *

Joe Harp was a violent place, but it was nothing compared to North Fork. There were around three hundred inmates in three cellblocks there, and they were all connected with a guardhouse in the middle.

That meant there was a lot of prisoner interaction, which can lead to frayed nerves.

North Fork also had a lot more gang activity, which is a huge problem in prison. A lot of guys are gang members when they arrive, and others join once they're there for their own protection.

The gang guys will tolerate each other most of the time, but the anger is always simmering. Raise the heat just a degree or two, and it may start to boil.

In these medium-security prisons, "home" is a large room filled with bunk beds—sixty, seventy, or even more. That's just too many for one room, no matter how big.

The guys are angry because they're locked down in there. They have no outside time. They barely get visitation. They're gang members, and in these close quarters, they tend to get in each other's way. They're black, Mexican, white—and they divide their space into their own little neighborhoods: this is the black area, this is the Mexican area, this is the white area.

This even happens in the bathrooms. This row of toilets is for the black guys. That row is for the white guys …

But when you put these guys all together, lines get crossed. There's bound to be trouble. Use the wrong toilet, and—BANG!—somebody's on the floor.

The gangs are always eyeing each other with a lot of distrust, and sooner or later something will happen. A couple of guys get into it, and the fight is on. And if you're in either gang, there's no watching from the sideline. Your job is to step forward and be part of it.

One morning at North Fork, I was in the common area when about twenty gang members got into a fight.

CHAPTER 9

The first one to get out of there was the guard. He left fast, which was smart, because if there's one thing both sides agree on in a gang fight, it's that they want a piece of the guard.

As things started to heat up, my friends grabbed me, put me in my cell, and locked the door.

They stationed a guy to stand outside my cell, and I told him, "They're not coming in here. They can't get in."

He said he was going to stay there anyway. He wanted to make sure nobody came over to start something with me.

Pretty soon, guards from all over the prison were on the scene. The pepper spray came out, and that ended it.

Now here's the crazy part:

You actually get used to this stuff. Guys in prison fight … a lot.

But usually they try to do it out of sight. They'll push a guy into a cell and post someone at the door to keep others away and block security cameras and guards from seeing what's going on.

Wait a little while, and the guy comes out bloody and bruised.

And that's the end of it. That's how they settle their differences.

* * *

Here's a rule to remember if you're ever in prison:

You don't steal from other inmates.

I had a radio in my cell. It was small and cheap, but I liked to listen to it—until it disappeared one day. Somebody stole it.

But it wasn't gone for long.

Pretty soon, one of my "protector" friends told me, "We know who got your radio."

"I'm not worried about it," I said.

"Well, we are," he said. "You don't do that when you're in prison."

My friends grabbed the thief, took him into a closet where they keep mops and stuff, and were getting ready to stomp him out when I said, "No, I don't want this on my conscience. Get him out of here."

I got a guard, and he hauled him off before he got hurt.

We never saw the guy again, which was probably a good thing—for him.

Another time, I was standing in line to get dinner, and some guy started opening his big mouth at me, saying stuff like "Once a cop, always a cop."

My friends decided to debate this assertion with him, so they grabbed him around the neck, pulled him off the line, and dragged him down to the shower, where they had a very serious intellectual discussion about his behavior.

I was kept out of it, so I couldn't see exactly what was going on—but I had a pretty good idea. He got the message. After that, he avoided me like I had smallpox.

I was lucky. I treated people well, and I made friends who chose to protect me. The younger guys will take advantage of older guys or disabled guys, but they came to understand that if they took advantage of me, they'd be sorry. If they stole from me, if they bad-mouthed me, it wouldn't end well.

* * *

So that's the first thing the governor and the sheriff and the warden will learn if they spend a couple of weeks in prison:

Violence is routine. It's part of the program. It comes with the sentence.

Prisoners fight, sometimes to the death. They'll stab each other. They'll bludgeon each other. Hopefully, it happens around you and not *to* you—but even if you're not a part of it, you're going to see it.

CHAPTER 9

I don't know if there's a way to eliminate it, because we send violent people to jail. But I'm pretty sure there are ways to reduce it.

All we really need is money—and lots of it.

The first thing we need to do is hire more guards. Lots of guards. And we need to pay them a lot more than we're paying them now, because, as the saying goes, you get what you pay for.

And right now, what we're getting is really bad, low-paid guards.

Prison guards are like cops. They're in a line of work that can be very attractive to the exact people you don't want doing it—men and women who aren't psychologically fit for the job. They may be mean; they may be excessively rough; they may be seeking the job to get even with something or someone. They may be exactly the sort of person—lawbreaking or law-enforcing—you don't want to see holding a weapon.

During my year and a half in prison, I came into contact with far too many guards who were just plain rotten people. They were mean, and their attitude and demeanor encouraged the violence they were there to control. They were simply wrong for the job.

If they didn't like something they saw, they wouldn't hesitate to grab an inmate, throw him on the ground, put cuffs on him, and haul him off to solitary confinement. But that's only going to make things worse, because solitary confinement can make you crazy. Nobody comes out of solitary a better man.

So if you want to reduce violence, the first thing you need to do is to hire good, decent, educated, compassionate prison guards—people who won't reflexively reach for their weapons at the drop of a hat and make a bad situation worse.

But right now, those aren't the guys who become prison guards.

In Oklahoma, guards get paid about eleven bucks an hour. You'd do better stocking shelves at Walmart or making Frappuccinos at Starbucks—if you could get a job there.

But if you can't … there's always an opening for a prison guard.

You sign up, you pass a medical exam, and, just like that, you've got a badge on your chest and a can of pepper spray at your hip—and you'll more than likely be on the job for months before you go to a class where you can learn about what goes on in prison.

I've actually heard kids talk about how they want to become prison guards because they want to shoot somebody or pepper spray somebody. And those idiots will get the job because the pay is terrible, the conditions are horrible, and there are lots of openings.

Here's what I learned in prison: the guards don't have a clue what they're doing. They're strutting around all proud of their new uniforms, they're young, and they know nothing.

They're untrained or undertrained, inexperienced, and underpaid.

They're just asking for it, and the inmates can size them up in a heartbeat. Then they get themselves into a jam, and out comes the pepper spray.

But pepper spray does more than sting your eyes and burn your airways. It actually contributes to the level of violence—because once that pepper spray clears, it leaves you in a very bad frame of mind. You want nothing more than to beat the hell out of the guard who sprayed it.

I talked to a sergeant who told me they used to administer a test to prospective guards that required some amount of intelligence. "We had interviews," he told me. "They were checking us for psychological difficulties, whatever, so forth and so on. It wasn't an easy job to get."

But that was a long time ago. I have no idea what kind of test we're administering now, but I know this much: whatever we're doing, we're doing it wrong.

We're offering lousy pay for a lousy job, and we're getting lousy people to do it—because we can't fill the jobs fast enough to meet our needs.

It's all about numbers. You put a guard in a prison yard with a hundred or more inmates, that's bad odds. But station a bunch of guards out there to watch those hundred or more inmates, arm them with batons and whatever else, and train them to use them only as a last resort—and you'll have less violence. I guarantee it.

But you'll have to pay them a real living wage, something they can support a family with, because this is not a job for bad people. If you want good people, you'll have to make the job more attractive. All it takes is money.

* * *

Another solution for reducing violence is to give the prisoners more space—and decent space.

Prisoners are generally young men who have a lot of testosterone, a lot of energy, and there's nowhere for them to release that. They rarely get to go outside—and when they do, they get herded into a courtyard that is filthy and disgusting even on a good day.

The drinking fountain is filled with bird poop. The toilet is filled with bird poop.

You wouldn't let your dog walk in that yard, but it's fine for your prisoners. It's not like they're human.

Now imagine what might happen if you tried treating them better.

There was an open area behind some razor wire at North Fork, and I got the idea that we could take down the wire, plant herbs and vegetables out there, and have a small group of guys go out and weed it every day. They even had an abandoned greenhouse out there that wasn't being used.

Wouldn't it make sense to give the guys something to do? Something they could be proud of? Wouldn't it be good to have them do this work and improve our food?

It seemed like a good idea to me. But nobody listens to prisoners with good ideas.

* * *

Vocational training would be nice too. There's a state prison in Hodgen, in the eastern part of the state, that has an automotive school where you can learn how to rebuild a car transmission.

It's out in the middle of nowhere, so the inmates are very unlikely to escape. The chances are they'll get eaten by a bear or something if they try.

But some of the inmates actually *do* get out. They've proven themselves trustworthy, and they're allowed to take state-owned pickup trucks out to run errands and pick up supplies for the prison.

There are other vocational schools too. They teach inmates skills they can use, skills that will make it possible for them to say, "I have the potential to be better when I get out of here than I was when I came in."

And here's one more thing to think about ...

In Oklahoma, you have all this labor potential sitting in prison. There's a large population of men who are doing nothing, and some of them are relatively stable and can do just about anything.

I talked to some guys who were in prison back in the fifties, and they said they used to let as many as eighty or ninety of them out to pull weeds in the cornfields.

CHAPTER 9

There were guys on horseback, carrying shotguns, watching over them—but they were fine with that. They enjoyed what they were doing. It beat sitting in a cell staring at the ceiling.

Sure, some prisoners need to be locked up at all times. But they do better, too, if they can get out and breathe some fresh air once in a while. So put them in chains and let them go outside. You don't want to let them out of your sight—you'll need to put guards out there to watch them closely—but I guarantee you this:

If you let them get outside to do some menial work every day or every other day, they'll be much calmer when you put them back in.

* * *

You can do all of this. You can provide more living space inside. You can offer vocational training for more than a tiny percentage of the prison population. You can allow even the most dangerous criminals to get some fresh air outside the prison walls.

It will cost a lot of money—and there's no money in Oklahoma—but consider the cost of continuing to do what you're doing now.

Lockup is dehumanizing. When you stuff a man in a cage, lock the door, and do little more than feed him, you're treating him like an animal. And when you treat him like an animal, he's going to behave like one.

But one of these days, he's going to be released from prison. And he'll be back on the streets—possibly in your neighborhood. And if you've been treating him like an animal, he's going to come out worse than he was when you put him in. I guarantee it.

So when you're considering how much it will cost to help convicts become productive and less violent, make sure to weigh that against the cost of doing nothing, which produces men who are more violent when they leave prison than when they went in.

When you deprive people of everything, it just makes them want to go out and hit somebody.

Keep that in mind when you choose.

10

HERE'S A SAD AND AWFUL TRUTH: if Eric Harris hadn't died in 2015, there's a good chance he'd be dead today anyway. He was only forty-four when he died, but he was a chronic drug abuser with the heart, lungs, and vascular system of a man nearly twice his age.

Harris spent more than half his adult years in prison, and if there's one thing I learned during my year and a half behind bars, it's that prison is the last place you want to be if you hope to break a drug habit.

Meth, crack, heroin, weed … you can get just about anything you want in prison. If you were using on the outside, you can keep on using on the inside. Even if you weren't using on the outside, you might very well decide to start using on the inside—because what the hell else do you have to do with your time? You'll have a whole lot of days to get through, and drugs will help you get through them.

The only thing you won't find behind bars is the one thing you need most: a good program to help you get clean. The illogic to that is stunning.

* * *

I had a little time to kill one day—just like every other day—while I was at North Fork, so I decided to conduct an informal poll of the 117 inmates in my cellblock. I figured out that only seven of us—just 6 percent!—weren't smoking, inhaling, injecting, drinking, or popping something that they weren't supposed to have in their possession in the first place.

Drugs are forbidden in prison, of course, but they're easier to find than a healthy meal. And everyone—the inmates, the guards, the maintenance workers, and even the warden—knows it. They know drugs are rampant, but they don't care—because there's another thing they know:

The only thing worse than having drugs in prison is having no drugs in prison. A stoned prisoner is a calm prisoner. When the well runs dry—when the supply runs out for one reason or another—that's when the trouble starts.

So the people in charge don't really care very much if a prisoner is so messed up that he can barely lift his head to get out of bed.

But you should care—because that prisoner's sentence has an expiration date. He'll be back on the streets someday—maybe soon, maybe in your neighborhood—and he'll be a full-blown addict willing to do just about anything to get high.

I know this guy. I've spent lots of time with him. And all I can tell you is, after he gets out, you don't want to get in his way.

* * *

There are a lot of ways to smuggle drugs into prison.

I knew guys whose girlfriends came to visit them with drugs stashed in their vaginas. I knew guys with very obese mothers who'd come to visit them with drugs hidden under their breasts or between rolls of fat.

CHAPTER 10

They'd come inside for a visit, go to the bathroom, come out, and stash whatever they were hiding under a vending machine in the visiting room.

Some guys told me they'd been in a prison where the drugs came in by way of a Hail-Mary pass. The suppliers would buy a football at a sporting goods store, untie the laces, stuff it with plastic baggies filled with meth, and lace it up again. Then they'd find the guy who played quarterback for the high school team a decade or two ago, and he'd come out in the middle of the night and throw it over the fence. Touchdown.

But now that you've got your meth, what are you going to do with it? Need a syringe? No problem. You can get practically anything in prison.

Prisoners with diabetes use small, disposable syringes for their insulin injections, just like diabetics on the outside. They have to go to the nurse's station to get their shot—they're not allowed to self-inject in their cells, of course—and when they're done, the nurse drops the syringe into a locked box, just like at the doctor's office.

But because this is prison, you can bet the farm that the moment will arrive when somebody will break into that box and walk off with a supply of syringes.

Those things go for a hundred bucks a pop. Get your hands on four or five syringes, and you've got four or five hundred dollars.

If all of this sounds familiar, it should. You've seen it all before on TV or at the movies. Only this is real.

* * *

Prison has an economy all its own, and drugs are its driving force. It's operated by mostly black and Latino gangs who control what comes in, what goes out, and how things get moved about in between. They establish the price, they manage distribution, and they transfer the money they earn back out to the source to keep the drugs coming in.

It's Economics 101—the law of supply and demand. And because there's a limited supply and a lot of demand, it's a big moneymaker.

Some inmates have visitors who can give them money to pay for their drugs. Others are less fortunate and may have to borrow the money. But borrowing is risky because—just like when you're in over your head on a credit card—lenders insist on getting their money back.

It's worse, though, because there's no such thing as bankruptcy protection in prison. If you borrow money and can't repay it, you've got a big problem. After a couple of warnings, you may experience shortness of breath, massive bruising, and excessive bleeding. And you'll still owe the money.

Once you've sunk to this level, your only solution may be to approach a guard and beg to be put in lockup—solitary confinement—for your own protection. Chances are you'll get what you ask for—and that's the last anyone will ever see of you.

* * *

If the wardens are content to know that all this is going on, the prison guards and maintenance workers take things a giant step further. The gangs depend on them to help keep the drugs and money flowing. Without their cooperation and active support, drugs would not be nearly as prevalent.

Guards and maintenance workers in Oklahoma work for peanuts. They make about eleven bucks an hour—a paltry salary that leaves them wide open to corruption. If they have a family or a car or a home, how the hell can they make ends meet on that? They might as well wear big "Corrupt Me!" signs on their backs.

Their low pay gives them every incentive to make a little extra on the side—maybe even a thousand bucks, off the books—by looking the other way or by becoming a courier. All they have to do is stroll over to the edge of the yard in the early morning and pick up that football, bend down and pick up a small baggie someone pushed through the chain links, or "accidentally" leave the door to the nurse's station unlocked.

A thousand bucks is a lot of cash. It can pay the rent, stock the fridge, put a warm coat on your back, and buy a whole lot of happy meals for the kids.

You don't want to get caught, of course. But it's an irresistible temptation, a relatively low-risk opportunity for a guy living in a double-wide mobile home with a wife and two or three kids.

And the opportunity never goes away. The guards are in constant contact with the inmates, they have every reason to want to get along with them, and they often become good friends with them. They figure out quickly who's running the show, and they know they can mutually profit from working together.

So when your inmate friend comes up to you and says, "Do you want to pick up an easy grand? I need you to run down to the fence when you get here at six in the morning, pick up a little bag, and get it back to me …"

You have every reason to say yes. Do the job well, and it can be a regular gig. And besides, you really need the money. Do your part, and everyone's happy:

The warden's happy because things are relatively quiet.

The guards are happy because they're making good money—tax free—on the side.

And the inmates are happy because they're stoned. They could be stabbing each other and beating each other up, but they're too stoned to think about it. They're either asleep or lying on their beds, happily staring at the bottoms of the bunks above them.

I never would have guessed it when I was a reserve deputy, but drugs are a problem in prison only when there aren't any. The inmates can get downright ornery when there are no drugs to be found. It's when they don't get through that all the fights start.

* * *

So what's your poison?

Alcohol? We've got it.

Get your hands on the right ingredients, and it's easy to find an inmate who knows how to mix up a truly foul batch of ... well, I don't even know what to call it. They call it beer, but this is not your daddy's Budweiser. This stuff is nasty. I've smelled it, and I don't ever want to taste it. I'd rather drink sewer water.

But it's there. Take a bunch of oranges and a sack of sugar from the kitchen, and you can brew yourself a batch of booze that will have you staggering around until you fall flat on your back.

If you see four or five guys barely able to stay on their feet in the recreation area, you know what they've been up to. This stuff makes them crazy drunk.

Do you prefer weed? There was a lot of marijuana at Joe Harp and North Fork. I heard that there was a Mexican inmate who controlled pretty much all the weed coming into North Fork. He left before I got there, and the word was he went back to Mexico with more than a million bucks in his pocket.

But mostly there was meth.

Meth was the drug of choice while I was in prison. The inmates just loved it—they said being high on the stuff was an almost out-of-body experience. They tried many times to get me to try it—but I never did.

* * *

If prisoners used drugs only in prison, nobody would give a damn. The only reason anyone even cares is that they take their drug habit with them when they're released.

That's when everything goes south. They're back on the streets, they want their drugs—they *need* their drugs—and, inevitably, they start selling drugs.

The first thing they do when they get out is look for a job. But good luck with that.

A lot of my friends in prison shaved their heads and had tattoos all over their faces, lips, nose, and eyelids. How are you going to find work when people are frightened of the mere sight of you?

A lot of the Mexican guys had tattoos of stitches on their lips. I knew a white guy who had a giant swastika tattooed on his back, and a small one on his face, below his right eye. That doesn't go over too well with prospective employers.

After spending two weeks or so looking for a job, it finally dawns on them that they're not going to get one. They're broke, they're addicted, they've got nothing. They're on a one-way road back to prison, and they know it. And a lot of them are just fine with that.

I was talking one night with a guy who was about to be released, and he told me he had almost two hundred dollars in his savings account leftover from the canteen and whatever else. He said they were going to give him a bus ticket back to Tulsa, and he planned to go to a casino when he got there and make lots of money gambling.

"No, you're not," I told him. "You're gonna lose your money, is what you're gonna do."

I told him where he was really heading: to a little community not far from the casino where almost everybody is cooking meth.

"You're gonna go up there and get stoned," I said. "And then you're gonna get in trouble. You guys are gonna start cooking again, and you'll be back in jail in thirty days."

And then he said something that just blew my mind.

"What the hell," he said. "I've got two more."

"Two more" meant two more five-year sentences. He was still in his fifties, and he was fine with that. "I get three meals a day," he told me. "It's air-conditioned out here in the summer, and it's heated in the winter. What have I got to complain about?"

There wasn't much to say after that. I'm sure they're happy to have him back. By now, I'm betting he's down to one more.

* * *

I visited a rehab center in Tulsa once that had three hundred beds, all occupied by meth users, and an administrator there told me that meth was the most addictive drug of all the ones he'd encountered. He said patients would try to give it up six, seven, eight times—and they'd fail each and every time. Finally, they'd just give up and leave. Nobody knew what happened to them; they were just gone.

So when you consider how many meth users end up in prison and how hard it is to kick their habit on the outside, wouldn't you think the Department of Corrections would try to do something to get them off drugs before they're released? Wouldn't you think someone would open his eyes and realize that maintaining a revolving door doesn't do anyone any good?

Wouldn't it make sense to try to help drug users get clean instead of punishing them for using?

We're so busy putting guys in prison for possessing marijuana or meth or heroin, but we're doing nothing to stop them from going right back into business when they get out—because they're going in addicted and coming out just as bad or worse. And the revolving door just keeps on turning.

Just before I got out of prison, they came into my cell and did a shakedown. There were some guards at North Fork who thought I was in the drug business because I had guys around me all the time.

Inmates kept coming to me when they had stomach aches and diarrhea because I had the means to maintain a supply of Pepto-Bismol and other over-the-counter remedies. But the guards figured it had to be more than that.

I told them, "Guys, I used to put people in jail for drugs. I haven't changed sides. I'm still against drugs."

But I've changed my outlook on the matter—because what we have is a mess.

Most people in their right mind don't go out and murder somebody. That usually happens when they're on drugs or alcohol. But we're doing nothing to help them, which means we're not doing a hell of a lot to lower the crime rate.

If you want to stop the cycle, you have to drag the users out of prison and get them into some kind of treatment. It's not going to be cheap, but it might make our streets safer. It might even save some innocent lives.

And this brings us back to Eric Harris. He was a lifetime criminal, a revolving door—but he was also a human being, and nobody tried to help him. There were no drug rehab programs for Eric Harris. There was nothing to help him try to get his life together. There were no programs in or out of prison to help set him on a better path.

> **Maybe if we'd tried to help him—if we'd tried treating him with some empathy instead of punishing him—he might have lived a productive, longer life.**

If Eric Harris ever wanted to get clean, all we did was make it harder. We sent him to prison when he was young, and we kept sending him back as he got older.

Maybe if we'd tried to help him—if we'd tried treating him with some empathy instead of punishing him—he might have lived a productive, longer life.

And maybe—just maybe—I would not have been in a time and place where I was trying to subdue him and pulled the wrong trigger. Maybe we could have altered the course of history before I made it.

11

THE MEDICAL SERVICES UNIT provides direct medical care to over twenty thousand incarcerated inmates and oversees the medical care of DOC inmates housed in private prisons. There are four infirmaries to provide special medical care for inmates and the agency has a service contract with the Lindsay Memorial Hospital for more acute care that cannot be provided on-site. inmates are able to access specialty care through the University of Oklahoma Health Sciences Center, as well as local hospitals and medical providers as the need arises.

—State of Oklahoma Department of Corrections[40]

Tell it to Joe Johnson.

Joe was an inmate at North Fork. I didn't know him well, but I'd see him most days when we were outside in the recreation area.

One day he didn't come out. He'd been complaining for a while that he wasn't feeling well, and he stayed in his cell on the second level, across from the phone bank.

I was on the phone with Charlotte when somebody yelled, "He's having a seizure."

I dropped the phone, ran up the stairs, pushed a bunch of guys out of the way, and found Joe lying face-down on the floor of his cell.

He'd been stumbling to reach the speaker in his cell so he could let the guardhouse know something was wrong, but he never made it. He fell down and smacked his head. When I got to him, he was bleeding from his nose and mouth. I checked his pulse and found none. I was rolling him over to perform CPR when a guard finally showed up.

The guy just stood there, looking down at Joe, very clearly not caring if he lived or died. Mostly, he was pissed that I was there.

I pushed him out of the way, dropped to my knees, and told him, "He's a big guy. Get down here and help me move him around so I can get him on his back."

The fat bastard helped me turn him over—and then he stood up and told me, "You're not supposed to be in here."

"Well," I said, "I'm not going to just sit here while you people look at him. He might be dead."

I beat on Joe's chest and started doing chest compressions. I kept at it for a while, and I checked his pulse several times—but I never got anything going.

I finally gave up and noted the time. They ordered all of us back to our cells, locked us down, posted a guard in front of Joe's cell … and his body just lay there on the floor for about five hours, until a couple of investigators from the DOC arrived.

I called over a guard and asked him to let the investigators know that the body wasn't lying where I found it. "I moved him," I said. "I turned him over and straightened him up. I'll be glad to talk to them."

But they weren't interested in talking to me. They looked around a bit, and then they hauled Joe off. About a week later, someone told me they thought he'd had an aneurysm.

That was the end of Joe—but things were just starting for me.

CHAPTER 11

A few days later, some inmates told me that the guards were saying they'd get me for going into Joe's cell. And a guard told me they were trying to tack some more time onto my sentence for "interfering."

Well, damn right I interfered. I figured Joe deserved a shot at life, and I did what I could to give him one. I tried to keep him alive.

Things simmered down eventually, and one of the administrators told me, "Don't worry, nothing will come of it."

That was a relief, of course, but it wasn't very comforting. This was not about me, and it never should have been.

An inmate collapsed in his cell, I found him lying on the floor without a pulse, and nobody in authority cared enough to try to keep him alive. They were just standing around saying, "Do you think he's dead?"

I tried to help the guy—and for that, they came at me.

They should have come for Joe.

* * *

Tell it to Ernie.

That's not his real name, but he was a real person. He'd been in one prison or another for most of his adult life before I met him at North Fork.

Ernie was having a lot of problems urinating. He was in his fifties, and he wanted to talk with me about it because I'd had surgery for prostate cancer twenty years earlier, when I was roughly his age. I was pretty familiar with the symptoms and treatments.

He told me he'd been having problems for a while and that they'd sent him for some tests before he got to North Fork. He had all his records, and he showed them to me.

I could see that his PSA—prostate specific antigen—was elevated when he took his first test. About a year later, they tested him again, and his levels were higher. They did a few more tests, and each time his level was higher than the last one.

Ernie said he didn't understand what the test was for and what a high PSA level meant.

But I knew what it meant. It meant they should have sent Ernie for a biopsy to check for cancer long before I met him.

They should have, but they didn't.

"What you need to do," I told him, "is next time you see the doctor or one of the nurses here, you ask them to run another PSA test. And if the level is high, you tell them you need to have a biopsy done."

It took several weeks until he finally got to talk to someone—probably a physician's assistant—who told him she was dumbfounded that he'd never had a biopsy. She ordered one, and they took Ernie to the University of Oklahoma for the procedure.

Four weeks later, they told him what they found: prostate cancer. And they said it probably had spread.

After some more tests, Ernie came back and told me, "It looks like it's spread to my lungs and internal organs. I guess I'm not gonna last very long."

They performed surgery on him at the University of Oklahoma Medical Center, and he was a real mess when he came back.

I don't know if he's still alive, but if I had to guess, I'd say he isn't. I know for sure that the Oklahoma Department of Corrections waited far too long to help him.

*　*　*

Tell it to my cellmate, Jerome Ersland.

While I was at Joe Harp, Ersland suddenly lost sight in one eye. You don't have to be an ophthalmologist to know that if this happens, you need to deal with it immediately.

CHAPTER 11

"You may have a detached retina," I told him. "That needs to be looked at now, because it's something that can be fixed."

Three and a half weeks later, he finally got to talk to someone.

They took him up to the Dean McGee Eye Institute in Oklahoma City, and once he got there, the wait continued. They have cells in the hospitals where they treat inmates, and whenever you go in, they just lock you down for hours before anyone sees you. Because you're an inmate, you're way beyond last on the totem pole.

As it turned out, Ersland's retina wasn't detached. It was something else, and I don't know if they were ever able to repair it or fix it.

But if it had been a detached retina, they would have gotten to it way too late to help him. He just would've lost sight in his eye.

* * *

There was a guy in the psych ward at Joe Harp—a huge man, I think he played football once—who would get down into a lineman's crouch, spring out of it, and run as hard as he could right into a wall.

Then he'd get up, dust himself off, and do it again. And again.

The first time I saw this—I was being kept there for my own protection—I went out and told the guard that the guy was bleeding, and that he was really screwing himself up.

The guard said, "Don't worry about it."

I remember another inmate who was catatonic, a classic case right out of a textbook. The first time I saw him, he was standing just inside the door of the building, not moving at all, staring into space, oblivious of everything around him.

I'd heard about catatonia, but I'd never seen it before, and I was fascinated. So I sat down on a bench and watched him for a while, and he never came to full consciousness while I was there.

A couple of inmates passed me, and I said, "What's the situation?"

They said, "Oh, he does it from time to time. Don't worry about it."

* * *

Some of the inmates in the psych ward would throw trays of food around during the day, and they'd lie down on the floor and kick the doors at night.

Don't worry about it.

There was a guy two or three cells down from me who I heard had killed one of his relatives, and he cried a lot at night, and he kept repeating, "Momma, I didn't mean to do it."

He could barely talk, and he couldn't walk—somebody said he'd had an accident and injured his back. He would stagger around and fall down—and, for the most part, people would just step over him and leave him there, like he was furniture.

Don't worry about it.

* * *

I was walking along the sidewalk next to the fence one morning, and I came upon a guy who was all busted up because he'd taken a dive off the second story of his building. He didn't know why he did it, but he was out there in the freezing cold, sitting on the steps of the administrative building.

And he was buck naked.

"David," I asked him, "what are you doing?"

"Nothing."

It wasn't long before a whole bunch of guys were out there, laughing and pointing at him, and the guards finally came running down and made him put his clothes back on.

David was a real character. He tried to tell me once that kids shouldn't be allowed to have cats or dogs because they have diseases.

CHAPTER 11

He said the Navy was going to take over the United States. He was dead certain that it was going to happen.

But don't worry about it.

* * *

In the psych ward, abnormal behavior is normal. And the bottom line, always, is "Don't worry about it"—until things get out of hand.

When that happens, when an inmate gets violent … that's when the fun starts. They call in the Special Operations Response Team—SORT, for short—to control the situation.

It looks like a scene straight out of Star Wars—five or six men, all decked out in helmets and armor, carrying batons for poking and shocking and whatever else.

It looks like a scene straight out of *Star Wars*—five or six men, all decked out in helmets and armor, carrying batons for poking and shocking and whatever else. They get the call, and they get there quick—because they love it.

The SORT members storm into a cell, pin the inmate down, and keep him there until the nurse comes in with a syringe and shoots him in the ass.

And suddenly, everything is calm. The guy is flat on his back and will be that way for the next twenty-four hours or so. Problem solved.

A shot of Thorazine here, a dose of Haldol there—that's how they treat severe mental illness.

Don't worry about it.

I think there was only one actual psychiatrist or psychologist at Joe Harp and North Fork. The rest were social workers, and I actually timed them once as they came through to talk to the guys.

The first question they asked was always, "Are you taking your meds?"

Four or five minutes later, they'd be on to the next inmate.

That's not psychiatric care. That's a meet-and-greet.

* * *

The Oklahoma Department of Corrections can pat itself on the back and proclaim that it provides wonderful medical and psychiatric treatment to the inmates in its prisons, but the fact is that the level of care sits somewhere between lousy and nonexistent.

Just ask any prisoner.

You get a routine checkup once a year, you get a flu shot in the fall, and beyond that you're pretty much on your own.

If you're smart, you won't get sick. If you're not smart and you get sick, this is what happens:

First, you have to fill out a request form to see a doctor. You write down what's ailing you, and you put it in a box.

Then you wait.

A day or two later, they take your form out of the box.

And you wait some more.

After another day or two, they may come back and tell you that you filled the form out wrong, and you'll have to start the process all over again. If you're lucky—if you filled it out right—then you're on your way to seeing the doctor … in two to three weeks, by which time you've either recovered or you're dead.

That's how long it takes to get medical treatment—unless you have a heart attack or a stroke. That's like hitting the lottery. They'll fast-track you if that happens.

But even when you're finally all set to see the doctor, they make things hard. The medical office is located a few blocks from the prison, and you have to walk to it, no matter what. If it's raining out, or if it's freezing cold, or if you're having problems with your legs or your back, or if you're just too sick to walk … well, tough luck. If you want to see the doctor, get up and walk.

It's the same with medication. It doesn't come to you; you have to go get it.

In rain, in snow, in freezing cold, in blazing heat, you have to stand outside the nurse's station once or twice a day, for as long as forty-five minutes, to get your meds. The nurse is inside, warm and dry in the winter and cool in the summer, and she passes your meds to you through a window when you reach the front of the line. But in the winter, if you don't have insulated underwear and a stocking cap you can pull over your ears, well, good luck. It gets damn cold out there.

* * *

CHARLOTTE: *Bob has a bad back and needs an eggshell foam mattress pad to sleep. They wouldn't give him one, and I finally had to go to the warden and beg him to get one.*

It became a major undertaking. I was trying to tell him he has a bad disk in his back, he's seventy-four years old, he needs help, and they didn't want to give him a mattress—just like when they didn't want to hook up his CPAP at the Tulsa County Jail, just like when he needed a toilet seat at Joe Harp because the water would rise up to the top, and he developed a horrible rash from sitting in it.

They don't want to give these men anything. They just don't care.

* * *

I broke my glasses. They needed a screw and a new bridge, and I had to write up a note—everything requires a written note—requesting a repair. Then I gave them to a nurse so they could be fixed.

I got them back three weeks later, and they were still broken. They delivered a tiny screw and a small screwdriver, and I had to fix my glasses myself. Why did that take three weeks? Because it's prison.

* * *

I've been receiving testosterone injections since I had surgery for prostate cancer. Without them, I get very lethargic and just want to sleep all the time.

Nobody wanted to listen when I said I needed them, so I called Charlotte, and she went to bat for me. It took nine months, but she finally arranged to get me my shots.

The first few I had were given to me at Joe Harp, by a real registered nurse who did an excellent job. But then they sent me to North Fork, where the nurse didn't know how to administer it.

Charlotte called my personal physician and explained the problem, and he walked her through what needed to be done. So here I was, an insurance agent serving time for manslaughter, telling the medical staff how to deliver an injection.

OK, this is the gauge needle. This is how you're supposed to do it. Blah, blah, blah, now you take it over.

But the nurse still didn't have a clue about how to deliver an intramuscular shot.

She came in, and I said, "What gauge needle do you have?"

She said, "Twenty-three," or whatever it was.

I said, "Twenty-five would be better. Have you done this before?"

"No."

"Really?"

"No."

And she wasn't kidding. She jabbed that needle right into my sciatic nerve, and it hurt like hell.

CHAPTER 11

There was a nurse practitioner on-site, and I begged her, "Please, let somebody come down here who can give me a shot in the butt without hitting my sciatic nerve and making me yell."

They found another solution. They decided not to give me any more testosterone shots.

They wouldn't say why, but they didn't really have to. The reason was clear: because I complained.

That's how they manage things.

* * *

Depression was common under the circumstances.

I was convicted of a crime that I knew I didn't commit; I spent forty-seven days in the Tulsa County Jail, alone in a cell, allowed out only once—at two in the morning; and I was seventy-four years old. Depression is not uncommon in older people.

So what did my jailers do? They took away my depression medicine.

Don't ask why. That's just how they manage things.

When I told them I needed my meds, they told me, "We'll check on it."

Every prisoner knows what that means. It's code for "Tough luck."

If you have no toilet paper in your cell, and you ask a guard to get you a roll, he'll say, "We'll check on it." And the next thing you know, you're ripping up a shirt into small pieces because you have no toilet paper.

* * *

This is the quality of medical and psychiatric care in prison. But why should you—why should *anyone*—care? We're talking about criminals, after all. Who cares if they're mistreated? If you can't do the time, don't do the crime.

That's a familiar argument. And it's a very bad one, because I'll say this again:

Most of these guys will serve their time and be released from prison. And it will cost taxpayers a lot more to treat their medical and psychiatric issues after they've been released than it would have when they were in.

Most of these guys will have nothing but the clothes on their back when they're out on the streets again. If they get sick, they'll have to depend on Medicaid or, if they're old enough, Medicare. If things get really bad, they'll show up—maybe in an ambulance—at the emergency room.

Now … who do you think is going to pay for that?

If you don't have an ounce of compassion for these guys, you should at the very least have a pint of common sense. We're not going to just let those guys drop dead in the street. We have a very simple choice: pay more now, or pay much more later.

Keep in mind that, from what I've seen, most of these inmates use drugs, and most of them share needles. Many of them—I think *most* of them—have hepatitis. We can treat their diseased livers in prison—or we can spend a lot more to treat them after they get released and their disease has worsened.

Some of these guys have HIV. We can treat that in prison—or we can wait until they're out and treat the full-blown AIDS they've developed because we chose not to treat them when they were in.

If they're mentally ill, if you have a guy who is snapping, you can shoot him full of Thorazine or Haldol and lay him flat on his back—but you're treating the symptom, not the illness.

When that guy comes out, where do you think he'll be when he snaps?

CHAPTER 11

Maybe it'll be at a shopping center, or in a parking lot, or outside your kid's school. How long will you have to wait until the SORT team shows up? Who's going to be there to sedate him when he's in the middle of a crowded theater?

* * *

There's another reason not to neglect the medical and psychiatric needs of prisoners: if you tell them that they're worthless, if you say you don't care if they get sick and die … I promise you, they won't forget it.

If they don't feel well, if they're sick, if they're unhappy, if they're not getting good food, if they're not getting decent health care, if they think nobody gives a rat's ass about them, if they're convinced that more people want them dead than alive, if they wake up every day afraid that someone's going to kill them …

How do you think they're going to feel when they get out?

I promise you, they're going to be pissed off at anybody who has something they don't—and that will be pretty much everybody.

And if they're pissed off enough, they just might want to exact some revenge.

So, when it comes to medical and psychiatric care in prison, here's a final thought from a guy who's been there:

You have a choice. You can help that guy now, when he's in prison. Or you can wait until he's out, when he'll be sicker and resentful that you decided to wait.

It's an easy choice, I think.

12

I HAD NO DOUBTS about what lay ahead of me when I entered prison. I'd seen lots of movies, I'd read lots of books, and I'd been personally involved in putting many criminals behind bars.

I knew for sure I'd be stripped of my freedom.

I didn't know I'd be stripped of my dignity too.

Prison literally strips you naked from the moment you enter the gates. The first thing they do is order you to remove all your clothes, bend over, and squat so they can peer into your butthole.

And from then on, prison strips you naked figuratively, peeling away your dignity in layers, each and every day you're there. It delivers a message twenty-four hours a day: you are society's waste. You belong in hell. And now you're here.

You say the food is making you sick? Too bad. You don't deserve to be healthy.

Your fingernails are dirty and need to be cut? Wait a week or two. Maybe we'll get around to bringing you a filthy clipper that barely works and might give you a nail fungus.

Your hair needs trimming? Have a seat. One of your fellow prisoners will tend to your needs as soon as he's done with that guy with head lice.

Need to wipe your butt? Here's a roll of toilet paper. Use it sparingly, because it's the only one you'll get this week.

Want to make a phone call on a gruesome summer day? OK.

Want to take a shower too? Nope. Sorry. You can talk to your wife and stink of sweat … Or you can blow off the wife and take a shower. One or the other, not both.

You say the toilets are backed up, and there's shit coming up through the shower drain? Guess you should have made that phone call.

They call it a correctional institution, but it's a lie. There is no correction in prison. Nobody is seriously trying to help you find a better path. The system is designed to make you feel worthless. It thrives on making you miserable.

It degrades you; it dehumanizes you. It is death by a thousand cuts. It goes out of its way, every single day, to ensure that you will be a much worse person when you leave than you were when you went in.

* * *

Choices are for people who are free. In prison, you get no choices. You take what they give you.

In the case of food, what they give you is dysentery. Beyond that, everything comes in stages—a classification system that goes from Level One to Level Four.

* * *

CHAPTER 12

CHARLOTTE: *When Bob went to the assessment center in Lexington, they put him in solitary confinement for his own protection, and he was at Level One, which means you get nothing whatsoever.*

* * *

At Level One, what they give you is nothing. If you want more than nothing, you have to wait for them to move you up to Level Two.

Here's how the system works:

At Level One—if you're in a restrictive housing unit for disciplinary segregation or protective measures, as I was—you get nothing.

At Level Two, you can get items from the canteen. But you can't participate in team activities, hobby crafts, tournaments, or other activities.

At Level Three, you can participate in organized activities and hobby crafts for one hour each weekday or two hours on Saturday and Sunday.

At Level Four, you can participate in all organized activities on the recreational schedule.

Your progress up the ladder is calendar based. You start out at Level One, and in three or four months, if you've been a good boy and haven't had any behavior infractions, you'll finally reach Level Four. Now, at last, you can order up to one hundred dollars' worth of items from the canteen every week—if you have a friend or loved one who is willing and able to put money in your account.

* * *

CHARLOTTE: *When Bob was in jail—and this is the same case with all prisoners—he had nothing. The only rights they give you are the ones they're willing to give, and in the beginning, they don't give you any.*

They stripped him naked and put him in a cell, and I couldn't get him his medication or his CPAP machine. They barely gave him toilet paper. They gave him a toothbrush and a blanket with a hole in it and nothing else—not even a Bible.

When they sent him over to the reception center at Lexington, he still got nothing. I called before he got there, because I wanted to find out what was going to happen, and I spoke with several people who told me he would be locked in solitary confinement for a minimum of six weeks. No phone calls. No visitation.

I said, "Really? I'm not going to know what's happening with my husband for six weeks?"

They said, "No. He will be allowed nothing. We will give him a toothbrush and the basic necessities."

I said, "Well, I want to make sure he gets his Bible."

They said OK, and after several failed attempts, I finally got a hold of the chaplain and told him, "My husband needs his Bible. He wants to pray. Will you please take him a Bible?"

He told me he would ... but he didn't. Bob never did get a Bible.

But here's what is most upsetting:

I didn't know it at the time, but I was lucky. Bob had me and his daughters on the outside fighting for him. Most of the prisoners don't have that. I can't even imagine what they go through.

* * *

All that was just the start, a preview of what was to come.

I went from the reception center to Joe Harp just in time for summer, which is brutal in Oklahoma even on the best days. It was July, I was seventy-four years old, I was being held in solitary confinement, and Lexington had no air conditioning.

CHAPTER 12

I was lying on a concrete slab, sweating profusely, and I asked if I could call my wife.

They brought a phone to my cell, pushed it through the bean hole, and let me call Charlotte.

"It's stifling in here," I told her. "I can't stop sweating. I just sweat all the time."

After we hung up, I pushed the phone back out the bean hole and asked the guards if I could take a shower—and that's when I found out that I'd wasted it on a phone call. You get one or the other, not both, they said. Those are the rules.

I was still at Level One, and I had to fight my way up to Level Two. I had to sit in solitary confinement and stay out of trouble for a prescribed number of days.

And how many days is that, exactly? They don't tell you. As many as they feel like, I guess.

But you absolutely want to move up, because when you reach Level Two, you get to order from the canteen, and you get a little more visitation time. It doesn't sound like much—but when you're at Level One, it sounds close to heaven.

Once you're at Level Two, of course, all you want is to reach Level Three, because it has some great perks—like you can order more toilet paper from the canteen.

And toilet paper is precious. On the outside, you can buy a thirty-roll pack or two every day at any big box store. But in prison it's a luxury item—and it's always at a premium.

At North Fork, they give you one roll a week—and no more. There are no exceptions, even if you're sick.

One roll a week is barely enough under normal circumstances, but there's nothing normal about prison, where you're always one mouthful of bad food away from a bout with dysentery.

When you're battling dysentery, you're looking at one or two rolls a day, not one roll a week. So you have to weigh your options.

You can ask a guard to help you out, but good luck with that. Tell a guard you need another roll of toilet paper, and he'll say, "I'll get back to you"—and then you'll never see him again because the guards take great pleasure in lying to you. They want prison to be the most degrading experience of your life—and they'll do all they can to make sure it is.

You can buy more toilet paper from the canteen—if you can afford it. But I met very few prisoners who cared to waste the little money they had there on toilet paper.

If you're lucky, you might find a generous prisoner who has a few rolls stocked up and will give you one. (Once I reached Level Four, I bought many rolls of toilet paper just so I could help out other inmates.)

But if you're unlucky, and you have dysentery, and you've gone through your weekly roll of toilet paper, and the guards won't help you out, and you can't afford to buy any at the canteen ... What then?

You improvise.

You tear a T-shirt into pieces, wipe with it, and flush it down the toilet. And now you have a backed-up toilet that's flooding numerous cells and sending sewage water up through the shower drains—because some high-level geniuses decided that prisoners don't deserve more than one roll of toilet paper a week.

* * *

If you're particular about cleanliness and hygiene, you'd much rather spend a month living out of a bus-stop bathroom than spend a day in prison.

CHAPTER 12

Want toothpaste? You can get it from the canteen. Don't have any money? Too bad.

Want a haircut? Go find some guys who will take a little off the top in exchange for some canteen items, like a candy bar or some instant coffee.

The guys who cut my hair had two sets of trimmers, and they used them on everyone. You'd haul your chair into their cell, they'd cut your hair and trim your mustache, and then you'd get up, and the next guy would come in. But the trimmers never got cleaned, and if the guy before you had head lice … now you had it too.

Since you weren't allowed to have your fingernail clippers, you had to put in a requisition to cut your nails, and in a couple of weeks they'd get around to bringing you a dull pair that barely worked.

You had no idea where those clippers had been before. They were rusty and covered in crud, and you had every reason to worry about getting a fungus or nail disease—but you took what they gave you. They handed them to you and said, "Here you go," and there you went—because the alternative was nine-inch nails.

* * *

CHARLOTTE: *At Joseph Harp, Bob had … well, we still don't know what it was. He had these sores all over him. It was horrible, and he kept saying, "Look at these sores. What do you think is wrong with me?"*

I didn't have a clue. I still don't. It was just something you got in prison. Everything Bob touched was filthy.

* * *

You can get a great education in prison if you're looking for a doctorate in violent behavior and drug abuse. But beyond that, education is a joke.

They offer programs where you can attend classes, but each cellblock has 117 inmates, and they'll take only twenty people at a time.

They offer ten classes total and not very often. And they provide a grand selection: Character, Thinking for a Change, New Life Behavior, Marriage Prep, Victims Impact, Life Skills, Walk the Line, Anger Management, Celebrate Recovery, and Genesis One—whatever that is.

People go to these classes because they give you credits that will shorten your sentence. But that's pretty much all they're good for.

They post a sign-up sheet when they schedule a class, but they don't tell you before it goes up there. So the first twenty guys who see it sign up, and everyone else is shut out before they even know it.

I got shut out many times, but I did manage to sign up and attend one—Thinking for a Change. I sat there, doodled, picked my fingernails, and looked out the window. It was nice to think for a change.

They can't offer these courses all the time because they don't have enough instructors. And the instructors they do have are essentially unqualified—they give them a manual to tell them how to teach the classes.

Basically, I'd say they offer these classes to make themselves look good. Nobody gets anything out of them.

* * *

The prison system can be very gracious. Look at some of the stuff they let you have:

One pair of sneakers. One baseball cap. One coat. One pair of shorts. Shower shoes. And *seven* pairs of socks.

But you can't have a belt, and you can't have gloves.

You can also buy stuff from the canteen—as much as one hundred dollars a week, if you have someone on the outside who will keep

CHAPTER 12

putting money in for you. You can buy snack foods, candy, instant coffee, over-the-counter medicines like Advil and Pepto-Bismol, and personal hygiene products like toothpaste and deodorant.

The prices vary from prison to prison—a bag of microwave popcorn might cost three dollars at one and five dollars at another. And everything is marked up, so they make a good profit on everything. It's like buying popcorn at the movie theater.

You can even buy a television. It'll set you back three hundred dollars, but it's every bit as essential as your seven pairs of socks.

There's a little shelf that comes out by your bunk, and you can put the TV on it. It's small—about a thirteen-inch screen—but it works. And it helps you get through the day. It's a very valuable asset because not everyone can afford to buy one.

I watched the news in the morning and a couple or three shows in the afternoon. I'd say I had it on thirteen or fourteen hours a day.

You can get newspapers, magazines, and books—but your visitors aren't allowed to bring them in for you. Everything has to come in by mail so it can be approved in the mailroom before it gets to you. Magazines like Playboy are nonstarters. So was a book I wanted to read about the Attica prison riot.

There's a lot of other stuff you can't have too: clipboards, shaving cream, cologne, dress shoes, t-shirts that aren't white or gray, sleeveless undershirts, colored boxers, pants and denim jeans that aren't state issued ... It's a long list, and it extends to visitors too.

* * *

CHARLOTTE: *They say they encourage family visitation, but they go out of their way to make it hard. They tell you what color shirt you can wear, or what color pants, or what color dress. But when you show up, after driving three or four hours to get there, they'll tell you they changed it.*

You were wearing the right color when you left, but it's the wrong color now, and they won't let you in. I learned to keep a wardrobe in my car so I could go change into whatever they wanted for the day.

* * *

Sometimes, it seemed like they were depriving us of things we needed just to be cruel. There was a diabetic guy at North Fork who had a very bad back and needed a wheelchair. What he really needed was back surgery, but there's no way you'll get that in prison.

He was having a horrible time just getting around, and the guys would help him out when they could. But they wouldn't let anyone bring him his medicine. He had to walk to get it himself—and some days he just couldn't do it.

So when that happened, he just went without his insulin. I wrote some stuff for him to try to help him get a wheelchair, but he never got one.

There was one thing you were allowed to have, though. And I have to laugh when I think about it, because it made no sense whatsoever.

In general population, you could have sixty, eighty guys living in one big room, and each one would have a box for his stuff at the end of his bunk.

To keep others from stealing your stuff, you were allowed to have two combination locks—the heavy Master locks that you can buy at any hardware or drug store—to lock your box with.

They were good for their intended purpose—locking up your personal items—but they were even better—great, really—for their unintended purpose:

When the shit hit the fan, you'd take those locks off your box, put them in a sock, and knot it at the end. And now you had a prison-approved weapon that could do some serious damage.

CHAPTER 12

I saw an inmate swing one on the food line one night, and he connected. He clocked a guy, and he went down hard.

Those locks can kill a guy, but it's OK to have them.

Master Locks, yes. Shaving cream, no. I still can't figure that one out.

* * *

You learn to live without a lot of things in prison, but there's one thing you can't have that you never adjust to. It's the thing you miss most, the thing they take away that makes you angrier and more resentful every day you're without it.

It's human touch. It's love ... friendship ... a hug ... a kiss. It's people who care for you.

Prisoners form bonds out of necessity. They help each other because they're in hell together. But when you get right down to it, prison is every man for himself. Those bonds are formed to get you through the day, the month, the year ... But they're not for life.

The bonds for life are the ones you have with your spouse, your kids, your parents, your brothers and sisters, your close friends ... And you're deprived of all of those when you're in prison.

Your family, your friends—anyone you put on your "approved" list who is likewise approved by prison management—can come visit you once a week.

I was blessed. Charlotte and my daughters came every week.

But they could afford to come. They had a good car and more than enough money to drive three and a half hours to the middle of nowhere, and three and a half hours to get back home. Not everybody has the means to do that.

* * *

CHARLOTTE: *A lot of families give up on their inmate. Maybe they don't have a car. Or maybe they have one, but they can't afford to buy gas. Maybe they don't have any money to fill the canteen. So they just don't go out to see them.*

Every week, when Bob's daughters and I went to see him, there'd be about ten or twelve other families there with us—and it was always the same ones.

The other inmates never saw anyone.

And they made it so hard even to visit. At North Fork, it's a pretty long walk outdoors from the entrance to the visiting area. You're not allowed to wear a coat, so if it's cold or rainy, you're going to freeze or get soaked. Or both.

I remember one day, we had freezing rain, and a young woman came in with her baby—and they wouldn't even let the baby have a blanket.

That just isn't right. It isn't human.

* * *

I knew a lot of guys whose families just gave up on them. I'd hear them say, "My parents are coming to visit," or, "My sister is coming to visit," and then they wouldn't show up. And it was devastating, because they didn't know what happened to them.

If somebody had a car accident, you probably wouldn't know about it for days. Even if the guards knew, there was maybe one out of twenty-five who'd care enough to tell you.

Other guys would say, "My mom and dad don't have enough money to get the gas to come." Or, "They have an old junker with bald tires, and highway driving is too dangerous."

It was always something, and I'm sure it was the truth. But it was sad, because I knew how much I needed to spend time with my loved ones. And they needed it too.

CHAPTER 12

Too often, they just lost everybody. I noticed that a lot of them, after doing two or three prison terms, would phone their relatives, and their relatives would refuse the call. They just hung up.

And of the thousand cuts, that's the worst one of all. Because human touch means everything.

* * *

Every week, when Charlotte and my daughters said goodbye, I'd start counting the hours until they'd come back. You can't measure how much it means to be with somebody who knows you and isn't wearing a prison outfit, how much it means to talk about stuff at home and things that are going on outside the prison walls.

It's heartbreaking when they leave, because you want to go with them, and you can't. But it's so much more heartbreaking when nobody comes to see you at all.

* * *

CHARLOTTE: *It's so hard to sit in the visiting area with someone you love, see how sad they are, and know there's absolutely nothing you can do to help them. I can't even describe how horrible it is.*

It was so important just to hold Bob's hand. They don't want you to have any physical contact, but some of the guards will kind of turn their eye from it and let you hold hands across the table. I needed to see how Bob was, to see that he was OK, because I was so worried about him. That human touch—the simple act of holding hands from across the table—meant the world to us.

Bob would always look at his watch when we were there. He'd keep saying, "I only have two more hours ... I only have one more hour ... "

And after a few hours, it would be time to leave. And I'd walk out of there, and I'd see them putting him back in handcuffs and leg irons and taking him away, and I didn't know if I'd ever see him again.

It was agonizing for me, and so much worse for him. But for those few hours we had, it was so good just to be together.

And the most important thing is, it kept Bob alive. I really believe that. If he hadn't had visitors, I don't think he'd have made it. My husband is a very strong man, and to see them put him in chains and pat him down when he left ... there wasn't a day or night that went by that I didn't cry.

It was just absolutely horrible. So having that visitation, seeing that, yeah, he's still alive, he's going to make it, we're going to get through this ... you would have had to put me in prison, too, to keep me from being there.

* * *

Here's what the lack of human touch does to you. I've been alive for three-quarters of a century, and I never had a temper until I went to prison.

But I have one now.

Since I've been out, if somebody pisses me off, maybe cuts me off on the highway, I have a hard time controlling myself. My brain just snaps—and it didn't do that before I went to prison.

And if this happened to me, it can happen to all the others. If one of these guys moves into your apartment house or whatever, you don't want to cross them. You don't know what might light their fuse, and you don't want to find out.

The irony of all this is that I was the luckiest guy in prison. I'm well educated, drug free, and well off financially. I have a wife and two daughters I love, and they love me.

And I can say these things because, unlike most of the other guys I was in with, I won't be going back. Those guys can't say the things I'm saying because their words will follow them into their cell when they return.

CHAPTER 12

When I read my own words, I start having flashbacks. And when that happens, I just don't know how I survived. I'm still having trouble with it.

The lack of personal connection, the lack of family time, the lack of human touch … They're all part of it. That and the way they treat you in prison. They don't care about you; they don't care what happens to you. You're dead to them.

* * *

CHARLOTTE: *The general manger of my company, Sheila, called me one day and said, "There's a dog that I'm thinking about adopting, but it's basically been in a cage for eight years [a product of a puppy mill]. It's never been touched by a human, never been held, never been petted. It gets very fearful and tries to bite."*

And I think that's the whole point in all of this. Every prisoner should be treated like a human being. Locking a man or a woman away and leaving them year after year with no physical or mental connection is just as horrible as what they did to the dog. If you put prisoners through this type of treatment, when they are released they could react much like the dog.

13

MY RELEASE DATE was set for October 13, 2017, and as fall approached, I stopped counting down the days. I could see the light at the end of the tunnel now, and I started measuring time in hours, minutes, and seconds. They passed by in excruciatingly slow motion, but every second brought me closer to going home.

Charlotte rented a large van so she could drive to Sayre with my daughters and their husbands, and then all of us could be together on the ride back to Tulsa.

Everything was set—until suddenly it wasn't. I guess the State of Oklahoma loved having me around, because it decided to extend my stay at North Fork, all expenses paid, for six extra days.

All because they found a small slash in my mattress.

For months, I'd been sleeping on a standard-issue prison mattress along with a foam "eggshell" mattress that the doctor got me for my seventy-plus-year-old bad back.

I slept with the foam mattress on top of the standard one, until one of my friends got it into his head that I'd be more comfortable if the two were combined into a thicker and cushier one-piece mattress.

So one day, while I was making coffee for the guys, he decided to do me a favor. He made a foot-long cut along the seam of my mattress and started stuffing the foam pad inside it. By the time I saw what he was up to, he was almost done.

I said, "Do you think I'll get in trouble for that?"

He said, "Nah, I'll sew it back up."

And he did, except for a couple of inches, and then I just forgot all about it—until about three weeks before I was due to be released.

There were some guards at North Fork who suspected that I was dealing drugs out of my cell, because there always was a group of inmates hanging around in it with me. I wasn't dealing drugs—I was making them coffee and giving them Advil and Pepto-Bismol for their assorted prison-induced ailments.

But groups of inmates make guards nervous, and one of them got it in her head that I was a drug dealer—so she decided it would be a good idea to shake my cell down.

The next thing I knew, the guards were shaking down all 117 inmates in the block.

And when they got to my cell, they tore it apart.

* * *

They didn't find any drugs, of course—but they did find a four- or five-inch tear along the seam of my mattress. And now I was in trouble.

"It's no big thing," I told them. "We'll fix it."

But they were having none of that. They pulled the mattress off my bed, told me it was "screwed up," and wrote me up for damaging state-owned property.

"One of the guys was doing me a favor," I told them. "He put my mattress pad in there to make my bed more comfortable."

They were having none of that either, and they left.

CHAPTER 13

After a while they came back and asked me, "Do you plead guilty to tearing up property owned by the State of Oklahoma?"

I said no.

About two weeks later, a couple of guards—a Lieutenant Smith and a Lieutenant McGill—came back and asked if I still wanted to plead not guilty.

"Absolutely," I said.

Then they asked me, "Why don't you just plead guilty? It won't affect anything. It won't extend your stay. All it will mean is that you don't have to go to a hearing."

I didn't want a hearing. I didn't want any distractions. All I wanted was to go home—and if pleading guilty would make all of this go away, without having any effect on my release ... then OK, fine, I'll plead guilty.

They reassured me that it wouldn't make any difference, so I changed my plea to guilty. I thought that was the end of the matter—until a few weeks later, as Charlotte and my daughters and their husbands were getting ready to come and take me home.

That's when they told me I'd be staying at North Fork for six more days, because I was guilty of damaging state-owned property.

* * *

CHARLOTTE: *Bob called me while I was at work, and he said, "You're not going to believe this, they're not going to let me out."*

He told me what was going on, and I was so upset. I'd waited a long time for him to be released ... we had everything planned ... I was so prepared for him to come home. I got off the phone and I started crying and throwing things around my office. I broke down.

* * *

I couldn't believe this was happening. I called some higher-ups to complain, and they told me, "Well, you pleaded guilty."

I said, "Why don't you educate these morons who told me that it wouldn't affect my sentence?"

And they said, "Well, it does. They just don't know."

Remember this story the next time you hear authorities talking about how they want to cut back their inmate populations. The fact is, they're flat-out lying. They'll do anything they can to keep you locked up. That's just how the system works.

* * *

Thanks to a well-meaning friend and a torn mattress, I now had a new release date—October 19. But as the day approached, I was becoming very apprehensive about what I'd be walking into when I finally walked out.

From the day I shot Eric Harris until the day they hauled me off to the Tulsa County Jail, I'd been hounded day and night by protesters and the press. I was pretty sure they'd be right outside the prison gate in Sayre, waiting to ambush me the moment I walked out—and I wanted none of that. So about two weeks before my release, I spoke to the prison staff, and I begged them, "Please, let me avoid the news media."

They ignored me. I went to at least three different people up the chain, asking to be let out very early in the morning, while it was still dark, but they wouldn't say anything—until about two days before my release, when they told me the warden was worried about the media.

"That's what I've been talking about for two weeks," I said. "I just assumed I'd have to wait until nine or ten o'clock."

"No," they said. "The warden wants you to leave early."

I called Charlotte immediately to let her know.

CHAPTER 13

* * *

CHARLOTTE: *We headed out in the middle of the night, because Sayre is three and a half hours from Tulsa, and they wanted to release Bob very early in the morning.*

We got there a bit early, so we circled around to look for the media. And we found them. The warden said he ran them off prison property, but there they were—right across the street, with their telephoto lenses.

* * *

At last, my time had come. They took me out of my cell, handcuffed me, and escorted me to the visiting area. A young guard walked in with Charlotte—and then another guard said she wasn't allowed to be in there.

* * *

CHARLOTTE: *The guard was very nasty. I looked at the guard who was with me, and I said, "Well, he brought me in here." Bob was standing right there, and this guard started yelling at the young guard, saying, "You're not supposed to bring her in here. It's not authorized. I'm the one who's directing this."*

I left the visiting area and went back out in the hall, and there was a man standing there. He started talking to me about the news media, and I said, "Can I ask who you are?"

And he said, "Well, I'm the warden."

I just couldn't help myself. I said, "Ohhh! You're the one who's been taking such good care of my husband!"

But he didn't get it. He just said, "Yeah."

They finally let me back in, and they took off Bob's handcuffs. And we walked through the security gate. We were outside. He was finally free!

I had brought a big coat, because I didn't want the press taking pictures of Bob leaving prison. I held it over Bob's face as we walked to the car, and all they got was his bottom half. I was so happy about that.

The next day, the newspapers wrote that I arrived at the prison with a cadre of security guards. It's true I had people with me. But they weren't security guards. They were Bob's daughters and sons-in-law. The newspapers couldn't even get that right.

* * *

A year and a half after I left, I was going home.

What I remember most from our drive back to Tulsa is watching the sun come up as we drove east. Depending on where your cell is located, you don't see a whole lot of the sun in prison until later in the morning, when it gets above the buildings. So, for me, seeing a sunrise was a shock, along with some other things I saw along the road.

It struck me that when you've been locked up in a small room—even for "only" eighteen months—you forget what a lot of things look like, especially when you're older.

* * *

CHARLOTTE: *Bob was almost in a state of shock. He just sat there in the front seat, kind of looking around. And we kept saying, "Are you happy? Are you excited?"*

And he just would go, "Yeah, yeah"—like he couldn't believe that he was out.

* * *

Charlotte kept checking our security system on her phone—she'd set up a network of cameras she could access remotely, to make sure the press wasn't sitting out there waiting for us. When we got to our neighborhood, I could see that there'd been some changes in houses and whatever else, but we finally got home—just in time for a nice barbecue lunch Charlotte had planned for the family and some friends.

A few of my friends who'd been in and out of prison several times warned me before I left, "Don't get out of here and eat burgers and fries and a whole bunch of stuff, because you'll get sick."

I didn't listen to them, of course. I wish I had, though, because I ate all that food. And just like they said, I got sick.

* * *

Freedom takes some adjusting to after you've spent time in prison. You don't just leave everything in your rearview mirror and pick up where you left off when you get back home.

After you've been locked up in a cell, alone with only a small window to peer through when you hear doors opening and closing … after you've spent countless hours every week pacing because you're bored out of your mind and it's the only thing there is to do … after you've gotten used to having to ask permission to see a doctor or use the phone or take a shower … After you've spent some time in prison, freedom does not come naturally at all.

Just being in a large, open space feels unnatural.

We have a large walk-in closet, about twelve feet long and eight feet wide, in our house—and for a while, after I got home, I seriously considered sleeping in it. I forced myself to stay in our bedroom, but I think I would have been more comfortable sleeping on the closet floor.

* * *

CHARLOTTE: *Bob had nightmares when he got home. He still does, but they were especially violent when he first got out. He would start fighting in bed, screaming and kicking really hard.*

I would wake him up and try to comfort him.

And he'd say, "Someone was sticking a shank in me."

* * *

When everybody's out in the cellblock, and there's a hundred guys or more walking around, you don't know who's got a knife, who's in a bad mood, who might have it in his head that you looked at him funny, even if you didn't. So you get in the habit very fast of always looking around to see who's nearby.

I'm still doing that when I'm in a crowd. I'm uncomfortable. I'm looking around, even though I know nobody's going to do anything. Prison made me paranoid.

I spent 540 days behind bars, always at risk. And now that I'm out, I still keep my back to the wall whenever I can so I can watch everyone around me.

Prison takes a toll, and I don't know if I'll ever recover. I sought help from a psychologist who specializes in PTSD, and she told me I have it, no two ways about it. She said I can expect it to go on for quite some time.

I can't recall ever losing my temper before I went to prison. My employees never saw me angry because I wouldn't allow it. If something got me upset, I'd go get a cup of coffee, or I'd get in my car and go for a ride. I'd come back later, when I cooled off.

But now, it doesn't take much to set me off. I get pissed off real easy.

* * *

They don't give you a get-out-of-jail-free card when you get out of jail. Nothing's free. There are strings attached. In my case, it was six months of parole.

Seeing a parole officer once a week wasn't going to be a problem for me. But seeing one in Tulsa … That was going to be hard. On the

CHAPTER 13

day I shot Eric Harris, I became a pariah in my hometown. Any good I'd ever done there was now irrelevant. If I so much as opened our garage door to take out the trash, it would be headline news.

I'd spent my whole life in Tulsa, but now it was time to leave.

Charlotte and I owned a home in Vero Beach, Florida, and we decided we should move there permanently when I got out. That meant I had to make arrangements to see a parole officer there.

We sent the necessary paperwork to Oklahoma City, and they sat on it for a while—but eventually they gave us confirmation that I could move to Florida if I arranged to see a parole officer there.

* * *

CHARLOTTE: *As soon as we got the confirmation, I called the parole office in Vero Beach and spoke with an officer who said he'd heard of Bob and was willing to handle his case.*

But he told me, "You have to fly out here. I have to make sure you actually have a home and that you're going to be living with your husband."

Well, I had a home, and I intended to live in it with my husband, so I said OK and took the first available flight out of Tulsa.

And the moment I touched down in Florida, Bob called me from prison and said, "You gotta get out of there. There's a big hurricane that's going to hit Vero Beach."

Talk about timing ... Half of Florida was in departures, trying to escape Hurricane Irma, and here I was, standing in arrivals.

I had a very quick meeting with the parole officer. He came to the house, looked around, and he agreed that our home would be a wholesome environment for Bob. And as soon as he left, I did too. I rushed back to the airport and caught the last flight out.

* * *

I got out of prison in mid-October, and we planned to move to Florida two months later, after celebrating one last Christmas in Tulsa.

We were all set ... and then I got sick.

I'll spare you the details of my symptoms. All you need to know is that my colon was leaking fluids into my body cavity.

I ended up in the emergency room, and a couple of days later I went back to have surgery. The doctors removed about a foot of my colon, and they said they found a tumor about the size of a softball in there. Fortunately, it wasn't malignant.

I'll always believe it had everything to do with my diet in prison. The doctors asked me what I'd been eating, and I told them mostly Cheerios and peanut butter sandwiches—when I could get bread. When I couldn't, I just ate peanut butter.

My surgeons, unsurprisingly, said that kind of diet was not conducive to good health. They also said that if I'd stayed in prison for another month, I would have died.

* * *

The surgery was more than just physically uncomfortable. It had a serious side effect: it complicated my plans to leave Oklahoma.

* * *

CHARLOTTE: *Right around Christmas, a probation officer visited us at home in Tulsa and said, "I understand you're going to Florida." But now Bob couldn't travel, because he had to have surgery.*

After the surgery, his doctor told him he couldn't travel for another six weeks. He said, "We just did major surgery on you. You can't get on an airplane or anything."

We told the Oklahoma probation officer what was going on, and he was starting to get nervous. He kept calling and saying, "When are you leaving? I'm getting a lot of pressure from Oklahoma City to get you out of here, or they're going to revoke his right to go to Florida."

And then things went from bad to worse. After several weeks, the doctor finally cleared Bob to travel—and then my sister became very ill with cancer. We ended up staying in Tulsa so I could be with her.

* * *

It took much longer than we ever anticipated, but we finally left Tulsa in February. As soon as we got to Vero Beach, I met with my new parole officer, and he laid down the rules for the next six months: come in once a week, do not touch alcohol, do not leave Indian River County without permission. Another important rule, because we own a boat and like to go fishing, was to not go into international waters.

Those rules sounded easy enough, and, besides, I'd have to obey them for only six months. At last, I felt I could return to some sort of normalcy and get on with my life. With permission, I could even return to Oklahoma once or twice to clear up some unfinished company business.

And then the phone rang.

* * *

Before we left Tulsa, after the surgeons said I could eat real food again, Charlotte and I went out for one last dinner at one of our favorite restaurants. It's a big place with a large bar inside.

When we walked in, I saw a few friends at the bar. I hadn't seen them in a year and a half, and they motioned me to come over and say hi. I walked over to them, and we hugged and chatted for a while, and then I went back to my table to have dinner with Charlotte.

We ate our meal, and we left, and that was all there was to it—until a few weeks later, after we'd gone to Florida, when Charlotte heard from one of her friends.

* * *

CHARLOTTE: *I was on my iPad, and one of my friends messaged me. She wrote, "What the f--- are they trying to do to Bob now?"*

I messaged her back, "What are you talking about?"

And she replied, "Haven't you seen the video?"

"Ummm ... No. What video?"

It was a video of Bob sitting at the restaurant bar with his friends a few weeks earlier. It was big news, a viral video, in Tulsa.

* * *

Nobody ever bothered to tell me this, but in Oklahoma, when you're on parole, you are forbidden not only to drink alcohol but to be anywhere that serves alcohol.

On the night we went to the restaurant, there was a man at the bar—I think he followed us there, because what were the chances that he'd just happen to be there?—and he used his cellphone to videotape me sitting at the bar and eating dinner at our table.

He gave the video to the press, and then all hell broke loose. People were saying I'd violated my parole. Eric Harris's brother, Andre, went on TV and said they should bring me back to Oklahoma and send me back to prison, just like they did his brother.

Suddenly, just when things seemed to be settling down, even though I was 1,300 miles from Tulsa, I was getting very nervous.

The video clearly showed that there had been wine glasses at our table. And there was a good reason for that: Charlotte had a cocktail with her dinner, and the restaurant serves water in wine glasses.

But the press was having nothing of that. They said I drank several glasses of wine, which was absurd. Ask anyone who knows me, and they'll tell you I don't drink wine. I like the hard stuff. But on this night, because I was out on parole, I had no alcohol at all. Absolutely none. All I had was a couple of cups of coffee.

The people at the restaurant told me that the guy who shot the video was a friend of the Smolen brothers, whose law firm represented the Harris family. They said someone from the restaurant didn't like me and showed the guy our check. He pulled out his phone and took a picture of it when he saw Charlotte's drink on it.

> So much for going back to Tulsa to clear up some business matters. There was no way I'd be going back.

So here I was now, a few weeks later, feeling very unsettled in Florida. I didn't know that I wasn't allowed to take a seat at a bar in a restaurant, and now people were calling for me to go back to prison.

I called the bartender, and he said he was willing to testify that I didn't order any alcohol.

I called our server—she's an acquaintance of ours—and she said I didn't have anything other than water and coffee.

And I called my lawyer. He said to stop worrying. It was big news in Tulsa, but it would pass. And he was right. Nothing ever came of it.

But now I knew one thing for sure: so much for going back to Tulsa to clear up some business matters. There was no way I'd be going back.

* * *

I'm a Floridian now. For six months, I met with my parole officer every week. We had our last meeting in late summer of 2018. We sat and talked for a few minutes, we shook hands, and I got back in my car and drove off.

Now I'm free to do just about anything I want. I can travel. I can drink. I can fish in international waters. I can even vote, thanks to a recent change in Florida law. The only thing I can't do is possess a firearm. It's an automatic ten years in prison if I get caught with a gun, and I intend not to serve even ten more minutes. I was a proud gun owner once—I owned about twenty of them in Oklahoma—but the law is the law.

Besides that, there seems to be only one other thing I can't do—not because of any law but because of who I am and where I've been.

I can't help. I can't volunteer.

I'd like to, but I'm having a hard time finding a place that will let me.

There's a drug rehab center at Indian River Hospital, owned by Cleveland Clinic. I'd like to go there and counsel folks—young people in particular—about the effects of drugs, how they ruin families, and what happens when drug abuse lands you in prison.

I filled out a form to act as a volunteer, and they told me, "Nope. That won't happen. You're a convicted felon."

I talked to a church near my home that has a group of people who work with drug addicts, alcoholics, homeless people, and others in need. I told them I wanted to volunteer, but they never called me back.

I contacted Kris Steele, the former speaker of the Oklahoma House of Representatives. He's the executive director of a group called Oklahomans for Criminal Justice Reform, and I called to tell him I'd like to talk to some groups about my experience in prison.**

** Oklahoma's new governor, Kevin Stitt, has made a difference in Oklahoma's correctional reform since taking office in January 2019. He appointed new people to the stale pardon and parole board and released several hundred inmates that were considered no risk to society. Governor Stitt is off to a good start. We are praying he stays the course on this long-ignored issue. Governor Stitt has done more for prison reform than the last governor did in eight years.

CHAPTER 13

I talked with him one time, and then he made it very clear that he'd have nothing to do with me. I was a hot potato. After that, he wouldn't return my calls.

I've asked the sheriff's office in Indian River County if there's anything I can do—even just to come down and talk with prisoners after they've been booked. I've asked the pardon and parole office. But all those doors are closed to me. I can't find anyone willing to stand up and say, "Yes, you can help. We'd love to have you come down."

And it's not just me. It's happened to Charlotte too.

* * *

CHARLOTTE: *When Bob was in prison, I became a board member of a group called OK Cure—Oklahoma Citizens United for the Rehabilitation of Errants. It was formed to help families of prisoners and to be an advocate for prison reform.*

Bob told me he'd like to help out with prison reform when he got out. I brought it up with the organization's president, and he told me he'd like to have Bob as a guest speaker. So I discussed it with Bob, and he said he really would like to do that.

When we got to Florida, Bob spoke with the president on the phone and told him he wanted to tell the group what he went through in prison, and the president said, "Yeah, we'd love to have you come and speak."

We set a date, and we arranged to fly back to Tulsa. Bob was prepared to deliver his speech when, the day before it was scheduled, the president called and said, "Umm, I don't think this is going to be a good idea."

He told Bob that somebody told him Black Lives Matter was threatening to picket.

Bob had no interest in causing any trouble. He told him, "OK, I'm out."

The speech was supposed to be at the Hardesty Regional Library, and they pretty much said they didn't want him there. They didn't want the liability, and they didn't want the problem.

It was devastating because Bob didn't testify at his trial and he never said a word while he was in prison. He never had a voice.

Now he wants to talk about what happened, and they've shut the door in his face.

They pretty much asked me to resign from the board too. They thought having me involved with OK-Cure would hurt the organization, so I resigned.

* * *

Charlotte and I still haven't healed from what happened to me, and I'm not sure we ever will. The shooting of Eric Harris, the racial turmoil it sparked, my trial, my time in prison ... all of it was horrific.

We're trying to live the rest of our lives in peace. We want to heal and move forward. And we want to help others, in any way we can.

But what do you do when nobody wants to let you help? What do you do when there are others who can benefit from hearing your story, but they've closed the door and won't let you in?

I guess you write a book.

14

ON APRIL 25, 2015—twenty-three days after Eric Harris died—the *Tulsa World* published a story under the headline "2009 Internal Memo Details Investigation Critical of Robert Bates' Treatment, Training."[41]

The newspaper wrote:

A 2009 Tulsa County Sheriff's Office memo detailing the internal investigation into the training of a reserve deputy who mistook his gun for a Taser earlier this month, killing a man, has been obtained by the Tulsa World.

The 2009 memo—titled "Special Investigation"—looked at special treatment Robert Bates may have received and questioned his field training as a reserve deputy.

Tulsa County Sheriff's Office Maj. Shannon Clark said he could not confirm the memo's authenticity.

"No one (at the Sheriff's Office) has seen it," Clark said Friday morning.

Earlier this week, Clark said he had heard of "some type of internal review"[42] *ordered by a former undersheriff, but "the Sheriff's Office has no documented record of a report being generated."*

Another year would pass before I'd finally have my day in court, but now my trial would be a mere formality.

Eric Harris, a black man, died in the hospital soon after he was shot by Robert Bates, a white reserve deputy sheriff who was assisting in his arrest—and now the *Tulsa World* has dug up a secret, six-year-old internal report that says Bates never should have been assisting the sheriff's department in the first place.

I wasn't qualified. I wasn't fit to serve.

What would be the point of a trial? My verdict was already in:

I was guilty of the crime of being there.

It was all laid out in black and white—in a report that nobody in the sheriff's department seemed to even know existed … in a report on an investigation that nobody ever told me had been conducted.

Never mind that it had been buried in a file cabinet somewhere for more than half a decade. Never mind that it was filled with mistakes and inaccuracies …

In the three weeks since Eric Harris died, his shooting had become national news, and now a report had surfaced that "proved" I was unqualified to do the volunteer work I'd been doing for years.

All the drug raids and arrests I'd participated in before 2009 and in the six years since? Irrelevant.

All the criminals I'd helped put behind bars? Irrelevant.

All of it was irrelevant—because I never should have been a reserve deputy to begin with.

Now, suddenly, my chances of getting a fair trial lay somewhere between zero and none.

As it turned out, the report wouldn't be entered into evidence at my trial. But it didn't have to be. There was no way the jurors didn't know about it when my trial began. They'd have had to be deaf and blind not to have known what was in it.

CHAPTER 14

I have no doubt that the revelation of that report was the final nail in my coffin.

Stick a fork in Bates, he's done.

* * *

The worst part of it all was that the 2009 report—and the reports about the report—were wrong on so many counts.

It was pure crap—all of it.

And now I want to set the record straight, because I know there are people who read the report—or who read stories about the report—and decided that I was a buffoon and a dumbass. And I'm sure they'll think that what I'm writing here is just sour grapes from a bitter, old man.

And I understand why they might feel that way.

But maybe they wouldn't if they knew how misinformed they were.

That report was written ten years ago. It lay hidden somewhere until it surfaced four years ago. And my blood still boils when I look at it today—because I can't get over how much my "investigator" got wrong.

So, yes, I want to set the record straight. It's hard to know where to begin, but I'll try.

* * *

The report,[43] written by Sergeant Rob Lillard, was presented to Undersheriff Brian Edwards on August 12, 2009.

In it, Lillard wrote:

On July 27, 2009, at your request I began to conduct a special investigation. As per your instructions, the investigation consisted of two specific inquiries:

Was Reserve Deputy Robert Bates treated differently than other Reserve Deputies in the past—specifically any Ex-Officers that were brought on the Reserve Program?

Was any pressure exerted on any employees by supervisors to aid Reserve Deputy Bates in this regard?

It would have been nice if Lillard had bothered to ask me those questions, because I could have cleared up any misunderstandings he had on day one—but I had no idea that he was conducting this top-secret investigation.

And from what I can tell, nobody else did either.

Even Stanley Glanz, who'd been the county sheriff since 1989, said he'd never heard of it. And that was a real shame—because so much of Lillard's report was flat-out wrong.

Lillard pointed out, correctly, that candidates for reserve deputy positions "must meet the same selection criteria as full-time deputies," and that "selection elements will include written examinations and physical agility testing background investigation, oral interviews, pre-employment physical and drug screen, and psychological exam."

He reviewed my records along with those of three other similar candidates who were required to have met all the policy requirements, and he concluded that "given the inconsistencies of our practices Reserve Deputy Bates was not shown favor in the selection process."

Not shown favor. Except …

Lillard went on to point out that all four of us were required to complete and document 480 hours of field training, and that I had "completed the process via a letter … wherein Bates was credited with completing 328 hours."

And then he delivered his knockout blow:

"To this point, Bates only acquired 72 documented hours."

Only seventy-two hours? That was BS, plain and simple.

CHAPTER 14

The fact is ... I completed more than the required hours of training.

I have no idea why only seventy-two of my hours were "documented"—and I sure as hell won't see any corrections made to the report now that I've served a year and a half in prison ...

But that was just flat-out wrong. It was pure BS.

And ten years after Lillard wrote it, I still have one nagging question that I can't get out of my head:

If he wanted to know if I'd fulfilled the training requirements, why didn't he just come on over and ask me? I wasn't hard to find. I would have set him straight right then and there, and this report never would have been written.

It never would have been buried in the back of a file cabinet somewhere, waiting for something bad to happen that would give someone a reason to root it out and give it to the press—and the twelve men and women who sat in judgment of me at my trial never would have known about it, because it never would have existed in the first place.

Consider this too:

If I'd known back in 2009 that someone had conducted a secret investigation into my qualifications and had written such a negative report, I would have told the department to go to hell. I would have picked up my stuff and walked out in disgust.

I could have found lots of other places to volunteer my time and my money. But stupid me, I chose *them*.

Why would I—why would anyone—want to volunteer at a place where they were being secretly investigated, and where nobody would have the decency to bring the "findings" of a damning probe to them to determine whether they were truthful?

201

I could have found lots of other places to volunteer my time and my money. But stupid me, I chose *them*.

* * *

There's so much more.

On page four of the report, Lillard wrote that Bonnie Fiddler, an employee in the training department in the Internal Affairs office, told him that no staffers or supervisors had placed any "undue pressure" on her to do anything unusual for me—"other than Chief Albin instructing me to make a certificate for driver training for Reserve Deputy Bates."

Fiddler told Lillard it was the only time Albin had asked her to do something like this, and she did not believe I had completed the training.

Well, there was a reason for all that—and I could have cleared it up for them quickly and easily, if they'd only bothered to ask me.

Chief Albin, who was a certified driving instructor, asked Bonnie to make up a certificate for me because I actually *did* complete the training.

Albin took me out to Tulsa International Airport early one morning during my training period to conduct my driving test. There was a runway that was off-limits to large planes because it had been recently resurfaced—but it was OK to drive a car on it.

We spent two or three hours out there practicing pursuit driving—going eighty, ninety miles per hour, slamming on the brakes, skidding … the things law enforcement officials have to prove they can handle.

Now, keep in mind that we did this at Tulsa International Airport. They keep records of who goes in and out, and they have cameras monitoring the runways at all times. You can't just drive out onto the tarmac and start driving like a maniac.

CHAPTER 14

Anyone could have called the airport and asked if Albin and I had been there. Anyone could have reviewed the video records and seen the car we were in.

But nobody thought to do those things. Or maybe they did, but they didn't follow through.

All I know is that they didn't ask me about it. And they didn't ask Albin either.

* * *

My application to be a reserve deputy sheriff included several recommendation letters. I passed my background check, my psychological screening, and my three-hour written exam.

My personal physician—a board-certified cardiologist and internist—performed my medical exam, which included treadmill, eye, hearing, and stress tests. He also performed my drug screening.

From what I can tell, the only requirement I didn't satisfy was my oral interview. I don't remember taking it, but it's my understanding that the sheriff has the authority to waive it for a reserve deputy. Stanley Glanz and I had known each other for decades. I think he knew me well enough to forego the interview.

* * *

I could go on and tear apart the 2009 report sentence by sentence, but what good would it do? It's my albatross. It will hang around my neck for the rest of my life.

Anyone who read that report—and that means just about everyone in Tulsa—presumed that everything in it was the truth, the whole truth, and nothing but the truth. But it seems to me that uncovering the truth never really mattered that much.

People still ask me why I didn't finish my training—but I know damn well that I did. They ask me why I didn't take the driving test—but I know damn well that I did.

I'm rehashing all of this now, because it still matters to me. So many "revelations" in that report were just plain wrong, and nobody in the sheriff's department or at the *Tulsa World* bothered to root out the facts.

Anyone who read that report—and that means just about everyone in Tulsa—presumed that everything in it was the truth, the whole truth, and nothing but the truth. But it seems to me that uncovering the truth never really mattered that much.

And I wasn't the report's only victim either. When all was said and done, it led to the resignations or firings of several people in the sheriff's department.

Chief Albin was forced to resign. Captain Tom Huckeby, who was interviewed in the report, lost his job. Major Shannon Clark, Sheriff Glanz's right-hand man, got fired.

The report cost Glanz his job too. He was charged with refusing to perform official duty and willful violation of the law because he failed to turn the report over to the media, which had filed a legal request to see it.

Glanz, the longest-serving sheriff in Tulsa County history, ultimately pleaded guilty to a misdemeanor and was given a one-year suspended sentence. He was a good man, and he was forced to resign in disgrace.

But that wasn't all. The 2009 report had one more casualty: the entire reserve deputy program.

A grand jury was convened after the report was made public, and it turned out that there were almost no records about the reserve deputies.

CHAPTER 14

Records or not, it was a damned good program with about a hundred people in it. And they just shut it down.

In the end, I lost my freedom, the sheriff lost his good name, several others in his department got fired or were forced to resign, and a fine law enforcement program was abandoned—all because of a report that summarized the findings of a secret investigation that was conducted six years before I shot Eric Harris.

And it was BS. All of it.

* * *

CHARLOTTE: *Bob was crucified by the press. Once that report came out, it wouldn't have made a difference if Jesus Christ himself came down to defend him.*

He was a dead man walking. He was going to prison long before his trial even started.

Bob would come in every morning and say, "Well, I'm on the front page of the newspaper again. Look what they're saying about me now."

The press were like vultures attacking a piece of meat.

Bob is white, and he has money, so they called him a pay-to-play cop. He is a man with a good heart who was trying to help the people in his community, and they turned everything around to make him look guilty.

The press dragged Bob through the mud—a sacrificial lamb. They tried to ruin his reputation. And he's still feeling the effects. I think he always will.

Bob worked very hard for years to make Tulsa a better place to live—a town he called home. And this was the thanks he got.

15

ON MARCH 3, 2019, in the small town of New Hope, Pennsylvania, a police officer entered a holding cell and directed the burglary and assault suspect in custody there to remove his belt. As the six-foot-four, 240-pound construction worker did as he was told, "a white, rectangular object consistent with a drug baggie" fell from his waistband and landed at his feet.

A scuffle ensued when the suspect refused to back away from whatever it was that he'd dropped, prompting a second officer with a service revolver in his hand to enter the cell to break up the fight.

He shouted, "Taser!" and fired his weapon, shooting the suspect in his torso. The entire incident was recorded on video.

I'd like to tell you the name of the officer who fired the shot, but I can't. His name wasn't made public. The Bucks County district attorney reviewed the case and determined one month later that he had not committed a crime.

"After careful consideration, I have determined that [the officer's] shooting of arrestee Brian Riling on March 3, 2019, was neither justified, nor criminal, but was excused," District Attorney Matthew D. Weintraub wrote in a letter to the New Hope chief of police.

According to the press release issued by his office:[44]

Weintraub said the law excuses the shooting officer's conduct from criminal prosecution because of his "honest but mistaken" belief he was deploying his Taser at the time he discharged his service weapon ...

Immediately prior to the shooting, [Riling] had been arrested and charged with intimidation and retaliation against a victim, simple assault and related offenses stemming from an earlier incident March 3. He is also charged with burglarizing the same victim's home in mid-February.

The officer who shot Riling was aware of these two criminal episodes ahead of the holding cell incident, and had himself heard threats of violence made by Riling during a phone call...

These details are not provided as proof of criminal behavior on Riling's part, but to illustrate the mindset of the officer who shot him ...

The use of a firearm must be an officer's last resort, Weintraub wrote, and was not justified in this case. However, the letter continues, because the officer believed he was deploying his Taser and not wielding his service firearm, he did not possess the criminal mental state required to be guilty of a crime under state law ...

This investigation is considered closed and the matter concluded.

The officer in that accidental shooting retired two days before the DA's office issued its press release. I have no doubt that he'll never forget what happened and that he'll always feel horrible about what he did. I'm sure of this because I've walked in his shoes. No law enforcer feels good about shooting a man, even when it's necessary and justified.

He feels awful. But he won't be charged with manslaughter, he won't have a trial, he won't go to prison, he won't have a criminal record—and he won't be a pariah in his hometown, always looking over his shoulder, for the rest of his life.

He'll remain anonymous because he lives in Pennsylvania.

I wasn't so fortunate. I did the exact same thing that he did—I shouted "Taser!" and fired my gun. But I had the misfortune of doing it in Oklahoma, where they made me a celebrity. When your narrative is "Bad Cop Mistakes Gun for Taser, Shoots Unarmed Suspect," I'm your poster boy.

I was then, and I still am. CNN, in its writeup of the Pennsylvania incident,[45] provided a link to a related story titled "How easy is it to confuse a gun for a Taser?" And since every story needs a picture, it included a photo of a law enforcer who made that mistake and shot a suspect.

That was me. They used my photo. It's how I'll be defined from now on.

* * *

The State of Oklahoma dragged me through the dirt, and I'll never stop feeling the effect of it. I know in my heart that I should never even have been charged, let alone convicted and imprisoned—but now I have a criminal record that will follow me everywhere for the rest of my life.

I served my time as a model prisoner, and I completed my parole without incident, but I'm in the system, and I'll never get out. I'm a convicted felon. My record accompanies me everywhere I go, and it will for the rest of my life. I'll never be whole again.

Charlotte and I wanted to take a trip to Canada—but it turns out that I can't go to Canada. They won't let me in because I'm a convicted felon.

I spoke with some Canadian attorneys, and they told me, "You won't get ten yards into Canada. It won't take them ten minutes, once you get to the border, to look you up and see what went on. They'll turn you around, tell you to check with them again in five years, and send you packing."

Canada's a sovereign nation, and it certainly has the right to do that. But should I be treated the same in my own country?

I can't even get a volunteer job. I went to the hospital near my home in Vero Beach and asked, "Could I come in one afternoon a week just to wheel patients around?" I told them I could help out in the emergency room too. I'm not squeamish. I could transport the bodies of patients who didn't survive.

They said, "No. You're a convicted felon. It's the rules."

I went to the local mental health association and said, "You have a drug program here, and I've counseled a lot of drug addicts. I've got some beautiful letters from guys I helped saying, 'I'm still clean. You helped me. I got off of drugs. I'm running twenty laps at our track every day. I feel great. Thank you. Praise the Lord in what you've done for me.'"

They said, "No. You're a convicted felon. It's the rules."

I can't even go out for a quiet dinner with Charlotte or my friends anymore.

I went to a little bar and sandwich shop in Jenks, a suburb of Tulsa, and they asked me to leave. They refused to serve me.

I went with Charlotte to a birthday party at a restaurant we used to frequent in Tulsa, and I ordered a drink after we finished eating.

CHAPTER 15

The manager followed me outside and said someone had called the restaurant to inform them that I wasn't allowed to drink.

"Look," I said, "I'm not on probation anymore. I'm free to drink and eat wherever I want to."

Well ... almost wherever I want to. The manager made it very clear that he didn't want me coming back.

* * *

This should not happen to a man who spends his entire life trying to be a good neighbor and an upstanding citizen. I raised two daughters, I married a wonderful woman, and I built a successful business. I donated my money and my time to help make the city of Tulsa more livable—but now, because of an accident, I'm a pariah in my hometown.

Do I sound bitter? Do I sound angry?

Well, you bet I am. And you would be, too, if you went through what I went through.

You'd be bitter if the people you worked closely with turned their backs on you when you needed their help just to save their own skin.

You'd be angry if the press just made stuff up for the sake of a good headline.

You'd be furious if you were wrongly convicted of a crime and sent from one hellhole to another and then to yet another in the Oklahoma prison system, where they treat human beings worse than the vermin that run rampant inside them.

And you'd be livid if you were still living with the aftereffects of what you went through—the frequent nightmares, the unnecessary explosions of anger, the constant fear of being among strangers.

* * *

> **I'll have to live with all of this, every day for the rest of my life. But I can't live with the notion that everything I went through is OK for someone else. The Oklahoma prison system is a human disgrace, and it has to change.**

I'll have to live with all of this, every day for the rest of my life. But I can't live with the notion that everything I went through is OK for someone else. The Oklahoma prison system is a human disgrace, and it has to change. You can't call yourself a decent, caring human being if you're satisfied with how things are today.

People give lip service to making changes, but that's all they give. It's all talk. From what I've seen, there has been no serious effort, judicially or otherwise, to do anything more than say we need to change things. The only ones who really care are the prison inmates and their families.

The director of the Oklahoma Department of Corrections, Joe Allbaugh, has asked the state legislature for two billion dollars to build more prisons.

But that's not the answer. That just shows how much he doesn't understand the system he's in charge of.

The state of Oklahoma has the highest incarceration rate—1,079 per 100,000 residents—in the civilized world.[46] Isn't that enough? Or does Allbaugh want to build more prisons so we can raise it even higher? And what if we spend two billion dollars for more prisons, and they're still not enough? Will we seek money to build even more?

Building more prisons isn't the solution. That sort of backward thinking has to stop. We're spending millions upon millions of taxpayer dollars to incarcerate men and women, and we're placing them in training grounds for the crimes they'll commit when they've served their time and are returned to the streets.

That's just stupid. There has to be a better way. And I believe there is.

For a start, we can stop incarcerating nonviolent offenders. In the years 2005 to 2010, nonviolent drug offenders comprised nearly a third of new prison admissions in Oklahoma.[47]

That's right ... we take people whose crimes are nonviolent, and we put them in a place where violence is the daily occurrence. If they don't know how to fashion a shiv, we send them to a place where they'll learn not only how to make one but how to use it. That's a skill that might come in handy once they're back on the streets.

If they get back on the streets, that is. There currently are fifty-five prisoners, forty-nine men and six women, serving life sentences with no chance of parole—for nonviolent drug possession.[48] A lot of murderers will walk out of jail before those fifty-five get taken out in their coffins.

Here's another depressing statistic: in 2016, arrests for marijuana possession jumped 20 percent in Oklahoma.[49]

It costs the state an average of nineteen thousand dollars a year to keep a man behind bars.[50] I think that's money well (but not wisely) spent when it separates violent people from law-abiding citizens.

But nineteen thousand dollars for each nonviolent drug offender? That's just stupid—and that's something I was well aware of long before I went to prison.

In all my years in law enforcement, I never wanted to put anybody in jail for possessing a bag of marijuana.

There was one time I stopped a car and found 550 pounds of marijuana inside. "Guys," I said, "We've got to go to jail."

* * *

There's absolutely no gain whatsoever in keeping nonviolent people behind bars—especially when you consider that Oklahoma is always shouting to the rafters about how it wishes it had the money to support programs that are designed to rehabilitate prisoners, not just to punish them.

But even if there is no money, that doesn't mean you should quit trying.

There are people who are willing to volunteer to help rehabilitate prisoners, people who can help them learn a trade they can use after they've been released. They can be taught to train pets. They can be taught to cut hair, to be plumbers and electricians.

When Charlotte would visit me, we'd be sitting with all these other prisoners, and a lot of them would tell her that they didn't know what they'd do when they got out, but they wanted to be tattoo artists—because they were honing the craft in prison.

You can make good money as a tattoo artist on the outside, but you need a license to be one in many states. Now, what do you think the chances are that the state's going to grant a license to a convicted felon?

They're somewhere between slim and none, but that's unsatisfactory. It has to change. I think the states have to do some rethinking.

Our prisons have revolving doors, and you're not going to change that if you're unwilling or unable to think outside the box. All you'll be doing is spending money to spend more money—and making everyone's lives worse in the process.

Yes, there's a money situation. But something has to be done to train prisoners so they have more than fifty dollars and a bus ticket when they come out.

* * *

CHAPTER 15

When you put people in prison, give them ten- or fifteen-year sentences, and make violence, filth, and degradation their "normal" living conditions, they're going to be much more dangerous to society when they come out than they were when they went in.

They'll be angry and unskilled. And since they'll have no hope of finding a job, they'll have nothing to do but get angrier.

Only now they'll be much more skilled at hurting people, because that's one thing you actually do learn in prison.

So what's the solution?

You start by no longer putting nonviolent offenders in prison. You stop the leak before the dam bursts.

The next thing you do is figure out what to do with all the nonviolent people already in prison. We need a plan to help the prisoners who've been incarcerated for possessing a bag of marijuana and who've been separated from society for as much as thirty years or more.

We need to hire good people who can go in and teach them a skill, something that will make them feel good about themselves, something that will make them feel that "I'm valuable. I'm a worthwhile human being—even though all I've heard in prison is that I'm not. I've been treated horribly, but I can move on. I can train dogs. I can cut hair. I can make tattoos. I can fix broken plumbing.

"I don't have to go back to selling drugs when they let me out, because I have a skill that will earn me money."

* * *

We also need to do everything we can to keep prisoners connected with their families. Inmates need to see their loved ones—their spouses, their children, their parents, their relatives—so they know there's someone on the outside who's anxiously waiting for them to come home.

We build our prisons in remote locations, and for good reason—but that makes it very hard for families that don't own cars or that can't afford the price of gas to make the long trip to visit them.

So we need to help. If that means paying for school buses to transport family members to prison, it's well worth the expense.

And once the visitors arrive, we need to stop going out of our way to make them angry and miserable. It's not their fault that their loved ones are behind bars.

* * *

There was a journeyman stone mason in the first prison I was in. They had unfinished jobs that required bricks and stonework, and he had all the skills required to do the job. In fact, he could have taken eight or nine guys over there and taught them how to do the job too—"Here's what you do … here's what you use … here's how you mix things …"

He was a prisoner with a skill, and there were countless people around him who could have profited greatly from having him as a teacher—but there was no way the prison officials were going to go for that.

How could they possibly go for that? It made too much sense.

We had some inmates who were journeyman plumbers, and they came in handy when there was something that needed to be fixed. We had a septic system that backed up, and they went down and fixed it. They waded in human waste for about a week, and the prison wouldn't even buy them boots to protect themselves.

It would have cost a fortune to get a licensed plumber out there with backhoes and other heavy equipment to get the job done—but they didn't have to spend that, because they had prisoners there with the skills to do it. Wouldn't you think they'd be willing to spring for a pair of boots? Would it hurt to add a few hundred bucks to their canteen money as a reward for their hard work? At the very least, maybe enough to buy a pair of boots?

* * *

People ask me all the time, "What can we do to help the system?" and my first answer always is "Blow it up." Tear it down, start all over, and get it right this time.

Obviously, that won't happen.

But when I go on and tell them that the system's a mess, they always reply that they'd love to fix things—but there's no money.

I don't believe that. I think they're just not being creative. I can think of lots of ways to raise money.

How about raising funds through vehicle registrations? There are hundreds of thousands of cars registered in Oklahoma. Why not slice a buck or two off of every registration and put it toward prison reform? Add that to the money you'll save by not incarcerating nonviolent offenders, and maybe you'll find all the money you need.

At the very least, you could make our prisons more livable.

There are 764 prisoners in the Oklahoma State Penitentiary, the maximum-security prison located in McAlester. "Big Mac" has no air conditioning and no fans, and the temperature in the cells can top 110 degrees in the summer.

When that happens, I've been told, the inmates stop up the toilets to make them overflow. Then they take off all their clothes and lie down on the floor.

Nobody—no mass murderer or serial rapist—should have to live like that.

So the first thing I'd do is shut down the prisons, including McAlester, that are in terrible shape. Leave them to the rats, mice, and raccoons that already live there.

The second thing I'd do is raise the salaries of the people who work there. Right now, you have guards and maintenance people who are running to the gate regularly to pick up drugs, cellphones, and other contraband that have been left there—because they can collect ten times their daily pay to bring them into the prison.

These jobs need to be made more attractive to better-educated workers who won't be corrupted as easily. The only way to do that is by raising the pay structure.

The third thing I'd do is radically change the concept of protective custody. I don't even know why they call it that. They should just call it cruel and unusual punishment, because that's what it is.

We say we're putting people in protective custody for their own protection—but what we're doing to them is unforgivable. We lock them up in a cell, alone, with no one to talk to, for twenty-three hours a day. We let them out for one hour—still alone—into what is essentially a cage that they can pace in, like a captive animal.

And that's on the good days. If it's raining or snowing, they don't get to leave their cells at all.

Human beings are social animals. We need to connect with others. We need human touch. Take that away, and you can destroy a person. That's what happens in protective custody. If you literally want to lose your mind, I recommend it.

The fourth thing I'd do is try to knock some sense into people who say to me, "Why should I care about prisoners? Why should I give a damn about their conditions, or about the danger they're in every minute of every day? Who cares if they're shooting themselves up with drugs or stabbing or even killing each other? They're prisoners, the hell with them."

Well, I tell them, the reason you should give a damn is because prisoners are human beings. And most of them will be back on the streets someday. And if you don't care about how you treat them while they're in prison … if you don't care about helping them get off drugs and learn a trade when they're behind bars … then they'll be much more likely to take their anger out on you, or your family, or your neighbor when they get out.

You should care about them and want to help them now so they won't want to hurt you later.

I can't help but think sometimes that the reason we keep some people in prison is that we're gluttons for vengeance.

I've been trying to help a guy from Mexico who has pretty much lost all hope. I spoke with an attorney who does pro bono work, and he told me he doesn't have a chance in hell of getting out.

Now, this guy has a job waiting for him at his uncle's construction company on the other side of the border. Release him, take him across the Rio Grande, and I guarantee he won't come back. There's no logic at all in wasting taxpayer money to keep him behind bars in Oklahoma.

There are so many others who could also be released with no risk to the public. I know guys who committed violent crimes thirty or forty years ago, and now they've aged to the point that they can't hurt anyone anymore.

Many are elderly. Some are sick and dying. What good does it do us to make them remain in prison until they die? Are we doing it for vengeance? Does that make any sense?

It costs over nineteen thousand dollars a year to keep a single inmate in prison. You can essentially double that for the more than three hundred inmates over the age of seventy because of their medical problems. There are hundreds more with diabetes, which leads to other diseases. It costs taxpayers a fortune to treat these guys in the hospital, but we keep sending them back.

So maybe you don't care about how we treat our prisoners. But do you care about how much it's costing you, a law-abiding taxpayer, to keep them living in inhuman conditions that will cost you more to keep them alive?

And if all those aren't enough reasons to make you care, then I offer one final one that may motivate you to think differently:

You should care, because it could happen to you. Or your spouse. Or your children, or your parents, or your friends, or your neighbors.

I know this for a fact because it happened to me.

My record was squeaky clean. I never had so much as a traffic ticket. But I ended up in the wrong place at the wrong time, and I reached for my Taser, and I discharged my gun, and I ended up going to prison for it.

If it could happen to me, it can happen to you. You might reach for your coffee cup while driving your car and hit a pedestrian. You might be distracted by your cellphone and cause a deadly crash.

It can happen—and no matter how much good you've done in your life, there's no guarantee that it can't happen to you. We're all at risk every time we drive a car, every time we have a drink, every time we go hunting ... every time we engage in our normal daily activities.

You should care about how we treat our prisoners because you could easily become one of them, and then you'd want people to care about you.

* * *

CHAPTER 15

CHARLOTTE: *I met a woman who has a vision problem. She got into an accident, the other person was killed, and they're threatening to put her in prison. She's scared to death.*

You don't have to be a burglar, or a robber, or a murderer. You could just be in the wrong place at the wrong time when something unfortunate happens, and you can go to prison for it. And if you do, you'll become a number. Everyone will think you're a worthless criminal.

It could be your mother or your father, your spouse, your brother, your sister, your son, your daughter. It could even be you.

Bob went through a horribly traumatic experience, and he's still very hostile when he speaks about it. It ruined his life.

He lost his business. He lost a lot of friends. He has nightmares where he's kicking, and he says he's dreaming that he's about to get shanked or that he's getting ready to shank somebody else.

That's what prison did to him. People just don't understand what it's like to live in a place like that.

* * *

I'm burned out, I'm pissed off, and I'm frustrated as hell. And I want people to know what I went through because I think it's important.

I really don't know if things can change. Most often, I don't see it ever happening because people just don't care enough to do anything about it.

There's a part of me that wants nothing more than to go off to Florida and forget all about it. But I don't think I'll ever be able to do that because it still bothers the hell out of me.

I'm sorry that I shot Eric Harris. I feel awful about it. I didn't mean to do it. It just happened.

The sheriff's department, trying to save its own ass, did everything it could to bury mine. And the press did everything it could to sell papers and garner clicks. They lied, they didn't check their facts … Sometimes it felt like they just sat down at their computers and wrote whatever they felt like writing.

It started the day after I shot Eric Harris. A reporter from the *Tulsa World* called me at home and said, "I'd like to talk about that."

"Under the advice of my attorney," I said, "I cannot speak with you."

I hung up the phone—and the next day, I opened the paper, and on the front page of the second section there was a story where the reporter said he'd gotten an exclusive interview with me.

The press said I was fired from the Tulsa Police Department in the '60s. If they'd bothered to check, they would have learned that I resigned. They lied about my training. They published the 2009 report and didn't care enough to find out if what was in it was true.

They said I bought gifts, including a Mercedes-Benz, vacations, and Rolex watches, to try to influence some people.

Well, stop the presses. I do recall taking a couple of watches off my wrist and giving them to some deputies who said they liked them. But they weren't Rolexes. They were Timex watches. I paid thirty-nine dollars for one and forty-nine dollars for the other.

I was the victim of lies and duplicity every day from the moment I shot Eric Harris until the jury declared me guilty. There's nothing I can do but live with that—but it isn't easy.

I always liked to talk to people, but now I just don't trust them anymore. Before I went to prison, I saw the press lie and the sheriff's department lie. And once I got to prison, I saw everyone in an official capacity lie.

CHAPTER 15

I've lost my faith in people. I'd like to get it back someday. That's what prison does to a man.

* * *

CHARLOTTE: *Nothing good came from this. Not for Bob, not for our family, not for Eric Harris's family ... nobody.*

Bob and I are deeply saddened for their loss and for ours. This was a tragedy for everyone.

If there's one thing we learned, it's what prison does to a man, whether it's Eric Harris or Bob or anyone else who's convicted of a crime and put behind bars.

We learned that nobody deserves to live in the squalor of a prison, or to experience the constant fear of being killed just for looking at someone the wrong way, or for owing a debt.

While Bob was in prison, a woman who worked for my company stole one hundred thousand dollars. The maximum sentence was ten years, and the prosecutors wanted to throw the book at her.

But I didn't. I told them I didn't want her to go to prison because of everything I'd learned about what happens to people once they're inside.

This woman had two small children, and prison was not going to help her one bit.

I told the prosecutors, "No, let's give her a chance to pay me back."

Before Bob went to prison, I'm not sure I would have said that.

But what happened to Bob changed my thinking. I know from what he went through—and from what I went through—that our prisons are not suitable for human beings. Not even for the worst of the worst. Nobody should have to go through what Bob went through and what I went through because of Bob.

And that's our goal. That's why Bob wrote this book. We want to make sure nobody ever has to go through this again.

PHOTO GALLERY

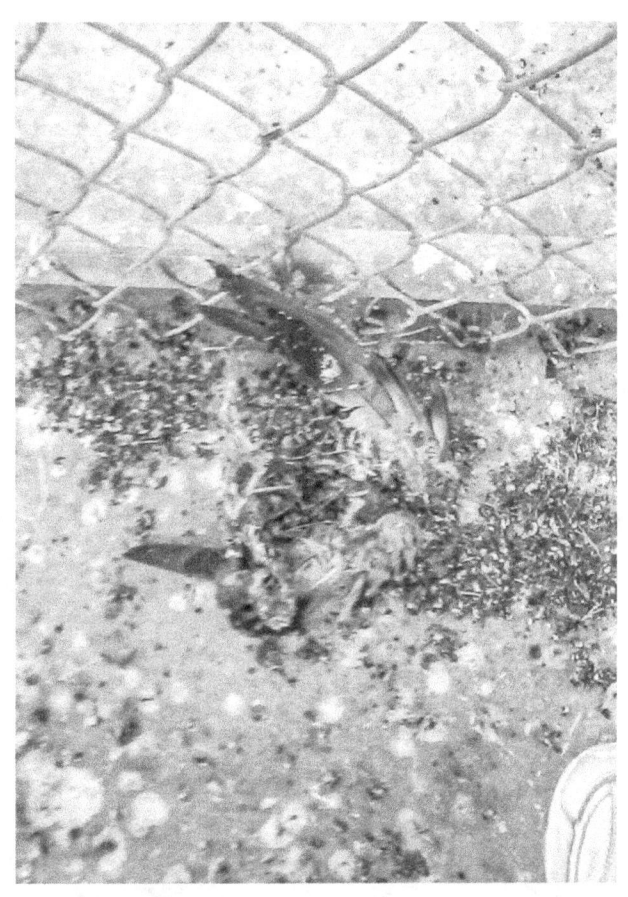

ABOUT THE AUTHOR

ROBERT (BOB) BATES was raised in Tulsa, Oklahoma, where he attended public schools. He attended Northeastern State University in Oklahoma and joined the Tulsa Police Department after he graduated.

Bob left the police force in 1965 to begin a fifty-one-year career in the insurance business. In addition to starting and selling two successful agencies during this time, he contributed to his community as a volunteer, maintaining his lifelong passion for law enforcement by serving as a reserve deputy with the Tulsa County Sheriff's Department.

He has two daughters, Leslie and Kathy, and six grandchildren.

Bob and Charlotte Bates have been married for twenty-nine years. They live with their dogs, Wallace and Pearl, in Florida.

ENDNOTES

1   Dylan Goforth, "Reserve Deputy Who Shot, Killed Man Thought He Drew His Taser, Release Says," *Tulsa World*, April 4, 2015, https://www.tulsaworld.com/news/crimewatch/reserve-deputy-who-shot-killed-man-thought-he-drew-his/article_67394595-5b09-59d1-a791-ae543e4cfcd1.html.

2   Goforth, "Sheriff's Office: Reserve Deputy Who Fired Fatal Shot Was Among 'Lots Of' Wealthy Donors in Reserve Program," *Tulsa World*, April 7, 2015, https://www.tulsaworld.com/news/local/crime-and-courts/sheriff-s-office-reserve-deputy-who-fired-fatal-shot-was/article_3d1f3fe7-43cd-5fa1-9e8c-d8b3aefe2504.html.

3   Editorial Editors, "*Tulsa World* Editorial: Time for a Thorough Review of Tulsa County Reserve Deputy Program," *Tulsa World*, April 12, 2015, https://www.tulsaworld.com/opinion/editorials/tulsa-world-editorial-time-for-a-thorough-review-of-tulsa/article_583b1431-004a-5275-b8cb-0b8d881f14a6.html.

4   Jarrel Wade, "Reserve Deputy Charged with Manslaughter; Family of Man Killed Says Response Mishandled," *Tulsa World*, April 14, 2015, https://www.tulsaworld.com/news/local/reserve-deputy-charged-with-manslaughter-family-of-man-killed-says/article_fbf44627-29c2-5c76-a972-eae344fa0b91.html.

5   Ziva Branstetter, "Protest Rally Draws Crowd, Ends at Tulsa County Sheriff's Doorstep," *Tulsa World*, April 15, 2015, https://www.tulsaworld.com/news/local/protest-rally-draws-crowd-ends-at-tulsa-county-sheriff-s/article_6405afb1-15e8-5c4d-87f7-0f61e4165a72.html.

6   Goforth and Branstetter, "Sources: Supervisors Told to Falsify Reserve Deputy's Training Records; Department Announces Internal Review," *Tulsa World*, April 16, 2015, https://www.tulsaworld.com/news/courts/sources-supervisors-told-to-falsify-reserve-deputy-s-training-records/article_a6330f10-a9fb-51e3-ab5e-4d97b03c6c04.html.

7   Corey Jones, "Friday Night Protest March Seeks Firings of Deputies, Targets Tulsa County Sheriff, Too," *Tulsa World*, April 18, 2015, https://www.tulsaworld.com/news/local/friday-night-protest-march-seeks-firings-of-deputies-targets-tulsa/article_650f7deb-de83-51f7-a6bc-894fd3653c08.html.

8   Goforth, "Tulsa County Reserve Deputy Apologizes to Slain Man's Family, Criticizes Reports of Impropriety," *Tulsa World*, April 18, 2015, https://www.tulsaworld.com/news/crimewatch/tulsa-county-reserve-deputy-apologizes-to-slain-man-s-family/article_8396c14f-e203-539f-a179-485c9a3724de.html.

9   Wade, "Reserve Deputy Charged with Manslaughter; Family of Man Killed Says Response Mishandled," *Tulsa World*, April 14, 2015, https://www.tulsaworld.com/news/downtown/reserve-deputy-charged-with-manslaughter-family-of-man-killed-says/article_fbf44627-29c2-5c76-a972-eae344fa0b91.html.

10 "Statement by Family of Eric Harris," *Tulsa World*, April 13, 2015, https://www.tulsaworld.com/statement-by-family-of-eric-harris/pdf_a30e41cc-5cc0-5b82-85e0-d6aa370de3f0.html.

11 Goforth and Branstetter, "Sources: Supervisors Told to Falsify Reserve Deputy's Training Records; Department Announces Internal Review," *Tulsa World*, April 16, 2015, https://www.tulsaworld.com/news/courts/sources-supervisors-told-to-falsify-reserve-deputy-s-training-records/article_a6330f10-a9fb-51e3-ab5e-4d97b03c6c04.html.

12 Eun Kyung Kim, "Tulsa Reserve Deputy Robert Bates Apologizes to Eric Harris' Family, Dismisses False Records Report," *Today*, April 17, 2015, https://www.today.com/news/tulsa-reserve-deputy-robert-bates-falsified-records-report-t15836.

13 Young, "Hundreds March for Justice in Downtown Tulsa" photo slideshow, *Tulsa World*, April 17, 2015, https://www.tulsaworld.com/photovideo/slideshows/hundreds-march-for-justice-in-downtown-tulsa/collection_9d3e687f-05ec-5a2d-aeb2-559794c52186.html.

14 Goforth, "Sheriff's Spokesman: Parts of Reserve Deputy's Training Requirements Might Have Been Waived," *Tulsa World*, April 17, 2015.

15 Wade, "Reserve Deputy Charged with Manslaughter; Family of Man Killed Says Response Mishandled," *Tulsa World*, April 14, 2015, https://www.tulsaworld.com/news/local/reserve-deputy-charged-with-manslaughter-family-of-man-killed-says/article_fbf44627-29c2-5c76-a972-eae344fa0b91.html.

16 Omar Villafranca, "Deputy Who Fired Gun Instead of Taser Was Investigated in 2009, *CBS Evening News*, April 22, 2015, https://www.cbsnews.com/news/tulsa-sheriffs-office-had-investigated-robert-bates-in-2009/.

17 Samantha Vicent, "Sheriff's Office Confirms Prior Internal Review of Reserve Deputy Robert Bates," *Tulsa World*, April 23, 2015, https://www.tulsaworld.com/news/local/sheriff-s-office-confirms-prior-internal-review-of-reserve-deputy/article_0b3693da-a9c7-5b03-9e72-71876c3297a8.html.

18 "2009 Tulsa County Sheriff's Office Investigation into Robert Bates," *Tulsa World*, April 24, 2015, https://www.tulsaworld.com/tulsa-county-sheriff-s-office-investigation-into-robert-bates/pdf_cdf59270-3033-5eaa-9e84-6975ebb5b3a5.html.

19 Vicent, "Murder Charge Dismissed Against Former Sheriff's Deputy Who Supervised Reserve Training," *Tulsa World*, August 21, 2015, https://www.tulsaworld.com/staff/ariannapickard/murder-charge-dismissed-against-former-sheriff-s-deputy-who-supervised/article_5ae10767-3131-5461-a67b-6189b3a6a9b2.html.

20 Wade, "Two Deputies Reassigned in Wake of Fatal Shooting by Tulsa County Reserve Deputy," *Tulsa World*, April 21, 2015, https://www.tulsaworld.com/news/local/two-deputies-reassigned-in-wake-of-fatal-shooting-by-tulsa/article_756c7584-c083-5eb2-bec6-9f864cbd7215.html.

21 Vicent, "Sheriff's Office Confirms Prior Internal Review of Reserve Deputy Robert Bates," *Tulsa World*, April 23, 2015, https://www.tulsaworld.com/news/local/sheriff-s-office-confirms-prior-internal-review-of-reserve-deputy/article_0b3693da-a9c7-5b03-9e72-71876c3297a8.html.

22 Wade, "Attorneys Demand Tulsa County Sheriff Release Report on 2009 Investigation of Reserve Deputy," *Tulsa World*, April 24, 2015, https://www.tulsaworld.com/news/local/crime-and-courts/attorneys-demand-tulsa-county-sheriff-release-report-on-investigation-of/article_440120c8-2791-5174-9863-2f3548720f79.html.

23 Vicent, "Protestors Applaud Possibility of Further Investigation into Tulsa County Sheriff's Office," *Tulsa World*, April 25, 2015, https://www.tulsaworld.com/news/downtown/protesters-applaud-possibility-of-further-investigation-into-tulsa-county-sheriff/article_e4549e6b-578a-5c8a-8b40-bf015d2134f4.html.

24 Wade, "Internal Investigation Focused on Top Deputies in Sheriff's Office," *Tulsa World*, April 25, 2015, https://www.tulsaworld.com/news/crimewatch/internal-investigation-focused-on-top-deputies-in-sheriff-s-office/article_d0217ad3-7d6d-556c-acd7-0ce11f5c57bc.html.

25 Wade and Kendrick Marshall, "2009 Internal Memo Details Investigation Critical of Robert Bates' Treatment, Training," *Tulsa World*, April 25, 2015, https://www.tulsaworld.com/news/crimewatch/internal-memo-details-investigation-critical-of-robert-bates-treatment-training/article_46c6c4a9-6f64-5c72-8c0d-7ba330cff67c.html.

26 Jones, "Public Scrutiny Over Robert Bates' Conduct, Training Puts Reserve Deputy Program Under Microscope," *Tulsa World*, April 26, 2019, https://www.tulsaworld.com/news/crimewatch/public-scrutiny-over-robert-bates-conduct-training-puts-reserve-deputy/article_b40ba2ed-8ee6-5246-90a0-719d0b0eaa19.html.

27 Jones, "Reserve Deputy Robert Bates' Age, Place on Violent Crimes Task Force Questioned by Expert," *Tulsa World*, April 27, 2015, https://www.tulsaworld.com/news/crimewatch/reserve-deputy-robert-bates-age-place-on-violent-crimes-task/article_0b28ec4d-85d5-5050-b798-e56b193d84bc.html.

28 Wade and Shannon Muchmore, "Autopsy: Eric Harris Had Meth, Not PCP, In His System When Shot by Reserve Deputy," *Tulsa World*, May 13, 2015, https://www.tulsaworld.com/news/state/autopsy-eric-harris-had-meth-not-pcp-in-his-system/article_fcccbf9c-a5e9-5c54-9057-0b930587a5b2.html.

29 Jones, "Internal Audit: 64 of 112 Tulsa County Reserve Deputies' Files Missing Training, Qualification Records," *Tulsa World*, September 25, 2015, https://www.tulsaworld.com/news/local/internal-audit-of-tulsa-county-reserve-deputies-files-missing-training/article_bb8b2045-d51d-55a7-aa86-fb960413f34b.html.

30 Oklahoma Uniform Jury Instructions, Criminal 2nd Edition, "OUJI-CR 4-104, Manslaughter in the Second Degree—Culpable Negligence Defined," OCCA Online, accessed September 16, 2019, http://www.okcca.net/online/oujis/oujisrvr.jsp?oc=OUJI-CR%20 4-104.

31 Arianna Pickard, "Second Judge Recuses from Robert Bates Case," *Tulsa World*, December 8, 2015, https://www.tulsaworld.com/news/courts/second-judge-recuses-from-robert-bates-case/article_120abaf4-3ad5-5080-8499-585cd3db1915.html.

32 Jones, "'Slips and Capture' Could Be Key to Robert Bates' Defense, but Expert Calls Concept 'Junk Science,'" *Tulsa World*, April 17, 2016, https://www.tulsaworld.com/news/local/crime-and-courts/slips-and-capture-could-be-key-to-robert-bates-defense/article_aacdd5e2-f85a-5d6b-9a61-3b3cf39bc965.html.

33 Force Science Institute, accessed September 16, 2019, https://www.forcescience.org/.

34 Jones, "'Slips and Capture' Could Be Key to Robert Bates' Defense, but Expert Calls Concept 'Junk Science,'" *Tulsa World*, April 17, 2016, https://www.tulsaworld.com/news/local/crime-and-courts/slips-and-capture-could-be-key-to-robert-bates-defense/article_aacdd5e2-f85a-5d6b-9a61-3b3cf39bc965.html.

35 Paighten Harkins, "Supporters Gather to Remember Eric Harris on Eve of Bates' Manslaughter Trial," April 17, 2016, https://www.tulsaworld.com/homepagelatest/supporters-gather-to-remember-eric-harris-on-eve-of-bates/article_4439a1dc-0620-5cff-9ab9-af38d241ae78.html.

36 "Robert Bates Jury Questionnaire," *Tulsa World*, April 19, 2016, https://www.tulsaworld.com/robert-bates-jury-questionnaire/pdf_4d5a1812-595e-5acf-98ae-3e37e90c556d.html.

37 Force Science Institute, "Force Science Explains 'Slips-and-Capture Errors,'" PoliceOne.com, July 22, 2010, https://www.policeone.com/police-products/firearms/training/articles/2144171-Force-Science-explains-slips-and-capture-errors/.

38 Pickard, "Defense Expert Witness Theorizes Stress Prompted Robert Bates to Mistake Gun for Taser," *Tulsa World*, April 26, 2016, https://www.tulsaworld.com/news/courts/defense-expert-witness-theorizes-stress-prompted-robert-bates-to-mistake/article_897d9be7-5f52-5254-ae7c-c73505e07772.html.

39 Excusable Homicide, What Is, 21 OK Stat § 21–731 (2014).

40 State of Oklahoma Department of Corrections, "Health Services, Overview," accessed September 16, 2019, http://doc.ok.gov/health-services.

41 Wade and Marshall, "2009 Internal Memo Details Investigation Critical of Robert Bates' Treatment, Training," *Tulsa World*, April 25, 2015, https://www.tulsaworld.com/news/local/crime-and-courts/internal-memo-details-investigation-critical-of-robert-bates-treatment-training/article_46c6c4a9-6f64-5c72-8c0d-7ba330cff67c.html.

42 Vicent, "Sheriff's Office Confirms Prior Internal Review of Reserve Deputy Robert Bates," *Tulsa World*, April 23, 2015, https://www.tulsaworld.com/news/local/sherriff-s-office-confirms-confirms-prior-internal-review-of-reserve/article_0b3693da-a9c7-5b03-9e72-71876c3297a8.html.

43 "2009 Tulsa County Sheriff's Office Investigation into Robert Bates," *Tulsa World*, April 24, 2015, https://www.tulsaworld.com/tulsa-county-sheriff-s-office-investigation-into-robert-bates/pdf_cdf59270-3033-5eaa-9e84-6975ebb5b3a5.html.

44 Bucks County District Attorney's Office, "DA Finds New Hope Police-Involved Shooting Not Justified, But Excused," April 12, 2019, https://bucks.crimewatchpa.com/da/29567/post/da-finds-new-hope-police-involved-shooting-not-justified-excused.

45 Ralph Ellis, "Police Officer 'Excused' after Mistakenly Using His Gun Instead of His Taser to Shoot Unarmed Inmate in Cell, DA Says," *CNN*, April 13, 2019, https://www.cnn.com/2019/04/13/us/jail-shooting-no-charges/index.html.

46 Ryan Gentzler, "Accepting Our Highest-in-the-World Incarceration Rate Means Believing that Oklahomans Are the Worst People," *OK Policy Blog*, Oklahoma Policy Institute, June 19, 2018, https://okpolicy.org/accepting-our-highest-in-the-world-incarceration-rate-means-believing-that-oklahomans-are-the-worst-people/.

47 Gene Perry, "Action Items for Oklahoma: Criminal Justice," *OK Policy Blog*, Oklahoma Policy Institute, March 21, 2013, https://okpolicy.org/action-items-for-oklahoma-criminal-justice/.

48 Jennifer Palmer, "I Will Die in Prison for a Nonviolent Crime," *Oklahoman*, May 3, 2015, https://oklahoman.com/special/article/5415846/with-oklahoma-prisons-over-capacity-some-are-calling-for-reversal-of-harsh-sentencing-law.

49 Gentzler, "Arrests for Possession of Marijuana Spiked in Oklahoma in 2016. What Happened?" *OK Policy Blog*, Oklahoma Policy Institute, December 19, 2017, https://okpolicy.org/arrests-possession-marijuana-spiked-oklahoma-last-year-whats-going/.

50 Harrison Grimwood and Kyle Hinchey, "'Recipe for Disaster': Oklahoma's Incarceration Rate Now No. 1 in U.S., Study Finds," *Tulsa World*, June 7, 2018, https://www.tulsaworld.com/news/local/recipe-for-disaster-oklahoma-s-incarceration-rate-now-no-in/article_0561c981-5e48-51a0-812e-19c22b33f55d.html.

www.ingramcontent.com/pod-product-compliance
Lightning Source LLC
Chambersburg PA
CBHW062033120526
44592CB00036B/1909